Media Fellowship
International

Media Fellowship International

A Model Christian Outreach to the Entertainment Industry

Edited by
JEANNE C. DEFAZIO
and SUSAN G. STAFFORD

Foreword by Julia C. Davis

Afterword by William David Spencer

RESOURCE *Publications* • Eugene, Oregon

MEDIA FELLOWSHIP INTERNATIONAL
A Model Christian Outreach to the Entertainment Industry

Copyright © 2025 Wipf and Stock Publishers. All rights reserved. Except for brief quotations in critical publications or reviews, no part of this book may be reproduced in any manner without prior written permission from the publisher. Write: Permissions, Wipf and Stock Publishers, 199 W. 8th Ave., Suite 3, Eugene, OR 97401.

Resource Publications
An Imprint of Wipf and Stock Publishers
199 W. 8th Ave., Suite 3
Eugene, OR 97401

www.wipfandstock.com

PAPERBACK ISBN: 979-8-3852-4285-6
HARDCOVER ISBN: 979-8-3852-4286-3
EBOOK ISBN: 979-8-3852-4287-0
VERSION NUMBER 02/25/25

All excerpts from books in the Wipf & Stock and Resource imprints have been reprinted with permission from Wipf and Stock Publishers.

Scripture quotations marked ESV are from The ESV® Bible (The Holy Bible, English Standard Version®), © 2001 by Crossway, a publishing ministry of Good News Publishers. Used by permission. All rights reserved.

Scripture quotations marked NIV are taken from the Holy Bible, New International Version®, NIV®. Copyright © 1973, 1978, 1984, 2011 by Biblica, Inc.™ Used by permission of Zondervan. All rights reserved worldwide. www.zondervan.com

Scripture quotations marked NKJV are taken from the New King James Version®. Copyright © 1982 by Thomas Nelson. Used by permission. All rights reserved.

Scripture quotations marked NLT are taken from the Holy Bible, New Living Translation, copyright ©1996, 2004, 2015 by Tyndale House Foundation. Used by permission of Tyndale House Publishers, Carol Stream, Illinois 60188. All rights reserved.

Scripture quotations marked KJV are in the public domain.

This book is dedicated to Pastor Bob Rieth,
his wife Marion, his daughter Renae, and his son Paul.

Contents

Foreword by Julia C. Davis | ix
Acknowledgments | xv
Media Fellowship International | 1
Those Who Attended Media Fellowship International Events Honor Pastor Bob Rieth | 19
Conclusion by Susan Stafford | 47
Afterword by William David Spencer | 59
About the Authors | 73
Bibliography | 81

Foreword
JULIA C. DAVIS

I am honored to participate in this project that pays tribute to Pastor Bob Rieth. High-profile members of the entertainment industry were members of Pastor Rieth's Media Fellowship International (MFI). In first-person accounts, each contributing author demonstrates great love for Pastor Rieth, describing him as a truly remarkable relational evangelist who was a powerful minister of Jesus's redemptive love. Media Fellowship International modeled ways to create Christian community in the media.

As an African American author and educator, I jumped at the chance to contribute to this book. MFI members and musical legends Billy Davis Jr. and Marilyn McCoo are wonderful role models for African American students. I recommend this book because it models inclusion and opposes the structural racism that prevents so many African Americans from reaching their God-given potential:

> Structural Racism in the U.S. is the normalization and legitimation of an array of dynamics—historical, cultural, institutional and interpersonal—that routinely advantage whites while producing cumulative and chronic adverse outcomes for people of color.[1]

---

1. Lawrence and Keleher, "Structural Racism," 1.

Foreword

Senator Jay Rockefeller took a public stand against structural racism.[2] Governor Jerry Brown signed the Racial and Identity Profiling Act of 2015 into California law.[3] Ahead of its time, MFI bridged the racial gap to bring the lost to Jesus. As a Christian African American woman, this really touched my heart. In the aftermath of George Floyd's death, it is important to mention MFI broke cultural barriers, acting out Acts 17:26–28 (NKJV):

> And He has made from one blood every nation of men to dwell on all the face of the earth, and has determined their preappointed times and the boundaries of their dwellings, so that they should seek the Lord, in the hope that they might grope for Him and find Him, though He is not far from each one of us; for in Him we live and move and have our being, as also some of your own poets have said, "For we are also His offspring."

I was honored to meet Pastor Bob Rieth at an MFI luncheon at the Waldorf Hotel in Washington, DC. The Holy Spirit and the love of Jesus guided that man of God. He saw the inside of people. I had the honor to write the foreword to *The Commission*. I am concluding this introduction with the beautiful message Pastor Rieth shared in *The Commission*:

> Loneliness is a disease of our time. Loneliness has nothing to do with the number of people in the room. In fact, we often feel more alone in a crowd. We are lonely when we have a hole in our heart that longs for companionship and understanding. We overcome loneliness when we have one or more relationships with people who care. Ultimately, we need to turn to our Lord and Savior for companionship and comfort. He has promised to be with us 24/7. "On my bed I remember you; I think of you through the watches of the night. Because you are my help, I sing in the shadow of your wings. My soul clings to you; your right hand upholds me." Psalm 63:6–8. Still,

---

2. "I've seen a lot of that and I know a lot of that to be true. It's not something you're meant to talk about in public, but it's something I'm talking about in public because that is very true." Everett, "Senators Duel," para. 7.

3. ACLU Northern California, "Governor Brown Signs."

Foreword

we need the presence of another caring person to dispel our feelings of aloneness and sadness. "This is why I weep and my eyes overflow with tears. No one is near to comfort me, no one to restore my spirit." Lamentations 1:16. This works both ways. Sometimes we are the ones in need and sometimes we are the ones that God will use to give comfort to others. We do not need to be trained counselors in order to be a comforter. We just need to be willing to be used by God to reach out in Christian friendship to those around us.

1. Be Approachable. Does someone who is hurting feel free to tell us his or her problem or ask us for help? Do we change the subject, tell a joke, or quote a Bible verse? Are we willing to share their pain or do we offer a platitude? Or, even worse, do we start to tell them our own problems, past or present?
2. Be Available. Are we so busy with our own lives that we have no time to see those around us? It does take time to listen and reach out to help someone. At the end of the day, what will count the most? Beware of the barrenness of a busy life.
3. Bear one another's burdens. Sharing the pain of someone's burden divides the pain and multiplies the relief. Even though we may not be able to change the situation, we can let them know that we care and share their grief. "Carry each other's burdens, and in this way, you will fulfill the law of Christ." Galatians 6:2.

Loneliness can trouble any of us. No one is immune. Remember these three helpful thoughts:

1. Jesus cares and has promised to be with us always. Let the presence of Jesus wash over us and comfort us. When we are content, we can be alone without being lonely.
2. We can comfort those in any trouble with the comfort we ourselves have received from God. Paul stated this principle so clearly in 2 Corinthians: "Praise be to the God and Father of our Lord Jesus Christ, the Father of compassion and the God of all comfort, who comforts us in all our troubles, so that we can comfort those in any trouble with the comfort we ourselves have

received from God. For just as the sufferings of Christ flow over into our lives, so also through Christ our comfort overflows." 2 Corinthians 1:3–5. We need to be receptive to the efforts of others to help us.

3. Be willing to accept the words and gestures of friendship from others. This reminds me of a song we used to sing in Sunday School: "Jesus and Others and You." What a wonderful way to spell JOY. With love and care, Pastor Bob Rieth.[4]

Terry McDermott's poem identifies the impact of loneliness:

> Does it matter what I do?
> Anyone care if I'm blue?
> Who will hear me if I cry?
> An invisible tear in my eye.
> Surrounded by people who do not see,
> I wonder if I'm really me.
> In a crowd I'm forever lost,
> Isolation at such a cost.
> A kind word would make my day,
> Help me find my way.
> Just to know that I am real,
> My broken heart would begin to heal.[5]

One of the greatest works of mercy is the gift of comfort. To accompany our brothers and sisters in all moments, but especially in the most difficult ones, is to practice the behavior of Jesus. He sympathized with the pain of others and offered the joy of the gospel.[6]

---

4. Bob Rieth, email interview, Sept. 20, 2020. In DeFazio, *Commission*, 45–47.

5. Terry McDermott, interview with Jeanne DeFazio by email, Nov. 28, 2024.

6. Mathis, *Jesus Among the Homeless*, 74.

Resources

Watch Julia C. Davis speak about her role as an educator at the Gordon-Conwell Theological Seminary's Boston Campus for Urban Ministerial Education (CUME) Chapel: "Creative Ways to Build Christian Community," October 6, 2016. https://www.youtube.com/watch?v=WKRN_XAvwHU.

Acknowledgments

Thanks to Carolyn Ridley for sharing her MFI photos and newsletters in this book. Thanks to Tammy Files for guiding me through the editorial process. Thanks to JoJo Starbuck for her encouraging words. Thanks to all the MFI members not mentioned in this book. Many thanks to Caleb Loring III for his support and to Peter Lynch for his kindness. Many thanks to Becky Norton Dunlap for reading the final manuscript and to Peggy Noonan for taking an interest in this project.

Media Fellowship International

Pastor Bob Rieth

"Media Fellowship International" was written by Jeanne DeFazio as told to her by Bob Rieth. This chapter was featured in DeFazio and Spencer's *Redeeming the Screens*, published by Wipf and Stock Publishers in 2016. Wipf and Stock holds the copyright to this work and grants permission for its publication as a tribute to Pastor Bob Rieth (1940–2022).

> Reverend Bob Rieth, founder of Media Fellowship International (MFI), has provided pastoral support, conducting prayer groups and counseling for Christians in the entertainment industry, for the past thirty years. The MFI ministry team goes on location to support the media during times of crisis: hurricanes, natural disasters, and crime waves such as school shootings and terrorist attacks. The MFI newsletter updates members about ministry outreach, prayer needs, and ministry events. MFI hosts a monthly meeting on a studio lot where Bob teaches from the Scriptures and prays for those in the media who attend. He meets monthly in Los Angeles

Media Fellowship International

with members of the media for one-on-one counseling. He respects the confidentiality of these public figures who need advice and support in crisis.

Here is his story: I was abandoned at birth and left in a garage to be found by a passerby. This birth circumstance turned out to be salvaged for good by the grace of God. A Christian couple, John and Ida Rieth, adopted me and I grew up on a small family farm near Valley City in eastern North Dakota. From an early age, my brother John and I helped with the milking and field work on the farm. John (who was also adopted by these godly people) and I both agree that the greatest blessing of our lives was being adopted into a loving Christian home. Daily, I counsel those who have made wrong choices because they were not reared with Christian values in a loving home environment. John and I attended Green School, a consolidated country school with ten grades. When I was fifteen, I attended evangelistic services with my family in our country church, Zion Lutheran, and accepted Jesus Christ as my Lord. I think the congregation may have been disappointed that week because I was the only one who went forward to accept Christ, but it has made all the difference in my life. At that time, I felt called by God to preach the gospel and lead others to Jesus. After college, I taught for a year, but knew that was not where I needed to be, so I attended the Association of Free Lutherans Seminary in Minneapolis, Minnesota. I was called to start a mission church near Seattle, Washington. My wife, Marion, and I moved to Kirkland, Washington, where we reared our family and worked together to build a new congregation: Our Redeemer Lutheran Church. In the 1970s, while serving Our Redeemer Church, I also ministered to the media in conjunction with Johnny Probst under the ministry name FCAME: Fellowship of Christians in the Arts, Media, and Entertainment. FCAME held monthly luncheons in the Marina City Club in Marina Del Rey, where members of the media were able to meet over an informal business lunch and hear testimonies of high-profile Christians. These events were often hosted by Susan Stafford, former *Wheel of Fortune* hostess, who is now part of the MFI chaplain

Pastor Bob Rieth

team. Top Hollywood stuntman Bob Yerkes, a member of the MFI Board of Directors, brought many celebrities to these luncheons: former Miss America Mary Ann Mobley and her husband, Gary Collins, and former Miss America Lee Meriwether and other friends of Bob Yerkes from his Circus of the Stars days. Famed actor, professional football player, and political hero Rosey Grier testified at the early meetings. Dale Evans and Roy Rogers became a part of the FCAME family during the 1970s. Peer mentoring was key to the evangelistic success of FCAME, which provided a comfortable atmosphere for celebrities to hear about Jesus from Christian celebrities. Many celebrities who otherwise would not have met Jesus did so through FCAME.

I founded Media Fellowship International (MFI) in the mid-1980s. MFI is a publisher of "glad tidings" in the tradition of Philip the apostle (Acts 8:5, 26–40; 21:8). In this account, Philip, one of the early church deacons, left Jerusalem and spread the gospel wherever he went, but, unlike most of his peers, he did not limit his audience to other Jews. He went directly to Samaria, the last place many Jews would go, due to age-old prejudice. The Samaritans responded in large numbers. When word got back to Jerusalem, Peter and John were sent to evaluate Philip's ministry. They quickly became involved themselves, seeing firsthand God's acceptance of those who previously were considered unacceptable.

In the middle of all this success and excitement, God directed Philip out to the desert for an appointment with an Ethiopian eunuch, another foreigner, who had been in Jerusalem. Philip went immediately. His effectiveness in sharing the gospel with this man placed a Christian in a significant position in a distant country and may well have had an effect on an entire nation.[1]

---

1. "As for Philip, an angel of the Lord said to him, 'Go south down the desert road that runs from Jerusalem to Gaza.' So he started out, and he met the treasurer of Ethiopia, a eunuch of great authority under the Kandake, the queen of Ethiopia. The eunuch had gone to Jerusalem to worship, and he was now returning. Seated in his carriage, he was reading aloud from the book of the prophet Isaiah. The Holy Spirit said to Philip, 'Go over and walk along beside the carriage.' Philip ran over and heard the man reading from the

Media Fellowship International

Like Philip's calling, MFI's special function is to carry the gospel to places in the media where it was previously unknown. Moving out of the traditional church into restaurants, hotel rooms, and studio lots provides a comfort zone for members of the media who are not comfortable in the traditional church. MFI takes advantage of every opportunity to explain the gospel. I reach out in taxicabs, planes, hotel concierge rooms, and over coffee in airport lounges. Metaphorically speaking, MFI puts sneakers on the gospel and takes it through the streets of Hollywood to its back lots, clubs, restaurants, and hotel meeting rooms. In the same way that Philip ran alongside a chariot to ask the Ethiopian if he understood a passage from Scripture, the MFI chaplain team follows the Spirit's leading, coming alongside people in the entertainment industry who are in need.

Michael P. Grace II, the grandson of New York Mayor W. R. Grace and an heir to the Grace trusts, sponsored several MFI meetings in Los Angeles and New York City. I spoke at Mr. Grace's Hollywood outreaches hosted in his home or in local hotels. I also preached at Mr. Grace's monthly meetings for the homeless in New York City from the late 1980s until Mr. Grace died in 1995. In the early 1990s, MFI hosted high-profile Christian testimonial luncheons sponsored by Michael Grace's organization, the World Alliance for Peace. Held quarterly at prominent New York locations, these luncheons highlighted powerful Christian testimonies from John Ashcroft (who later became the US Attorney General) and Martha Williamson, producer of *Touched by an Angel*, among others.

---

prophet Isaiah. Philip asked, 'Do you understand what you are reading?' The man replied, 'How can I, unless someone instructs me?' And he urged Philip to come up into the carriage and sit with him. The passage of Scripture he had been reading was this: 'He was led like a sheep to the slaughter. As a lamb is silent before the shearers, he did not open his mouth. He was humiliated and received no justice. Who can speak of his descendants? For his life was taken from the earth.' The eunuch asked Philip, 'Tell me, was the prophet talking about himself or someone else?' So beginning with this same Scripture, Philip told him the Good News about Jesus" (Acts 8:26–35 NLT).

Pastor Bob Rieth

The celebrity Christian testimony is a key strategy of MFI's practical theology. People can argue theology, but they cannot argue with a testimony, because our stories are what they are. Mr. Grace's friends from high society, the business world, and members of his family attended the MFI luncheons. Mr. Grace's cousin Morgan Grace; Tony Duke, founder of Boys and Girls Harbor; Monsignor Avery Dulles (who later became Cardinal Dulles), and Ben Bradlee, editor of the *Washington Post*, attended MFI's New York City luncheons. Mr. Grace's sons, Michael, Winston, and Zachary, and his daughters, Yvonne and Ginger, attended his Los Angeles meetings. His nephews William R. Grace and Joseph P. Grace attended MFI's Washington, DC, luncheons. These MFI meetings introduced people to Jesus because each meeting was conveniently located, and the testimonial speakers witnessed the gospel in a language the attendees could understand. Each testimony focused on Jesus's love and redemption in a way that was meaningful to the attendees' lives.[2]

Currently, I host a monthly meeting on the CBS studio lots teaching from Scripture and praying for those in the media. Former CBS executive Charles Cappleman attends regularly. I meet with members of the media at a San Fernando Valley restaurant teaching from Scripture after dinner. Wink Martindale and his wife Sandy, as well as Marilyn McCoo and Billy Davis Jr., dine with us

---

2. Pastor Bob Rieth commented on the impact of MFI New York City events hosted by Michael Grace in the book *Creative Ways to Build Christian Community*: He [Michael Grace] "had a burning passion to bring the gospel of Jesus Christ to everyone, especially to those who were either 'up and out' or 'down and out.' . . . Michael called on Media Fellowship International and Pastor Bob Rieth to help with this missionary effort. MFI is a ministry that reaches out to the secular media and entertainment community with the goal of introducing individuals to Jesus, nurturing them as they learn God's Word, and encouraging them as they walk with God in their professional and personal lives.

It was a privilege and a blessing to be able to partner with him to preach and to teach the saving Word of the Lord to the people that Michael invited in from the highways and byways to come and sit at the table and be fed the Word." DeFazio and Lathrop, *Creative Ways*, 11–12.

Media Fellowship International

often. I counsel high-profile members of the media confidentially and one-on-one each month in Los Angeles. Every year, MFI members attend the President's Prayer Breakfast in Washington, DC. MFI hosts a luncheon for members of the Metro-DC-area media at the Mayflower Hotel during that week. The Media Fellowship International Emergency Response Team was called to Columbine and Virginia Tech to counsel survivors and families in the aftermath of the shootings. MFI went to New Orleans to pray and offer spiritual support in the aftermath of Hurricane Katrina.

In April 2015, the MFI media support ministry team traveled to Israel when media members were covering the crisis in the Gaza strip, using relational evangelism to bring Jesus's message of love and reconciliation to the media covering this global crisis. Members of the press often risk their lives to cover terrorist acts and natural disasters. In these life-or-death moments, MFI offers critical spiritual support. At the time, there was a ceasefire in what was called the fifty-day war on the Gaza-Israel border. This trip was born out of prayer and deep concern for the people in the news crews in places of danger. We wanted to stand behind them and let them know they were being cared for. In light of the ISIS brutality, we realized we needed to pray urgently for them. Another purpose for this trip was to gather information on the possibilities for having a Media Support Team presence in the Middle East. We would be there to listen to them and talk to them individually, to pray with them, and to befriend them. I met a bureau chief for CBN in the Middle East, Chris Mitchell, who invited me and MFI to come at this time. We talked about what Media Fellowship could do to help and how we offered practical and spiritual support to be true to MFI's calling and purpose, expressing a willingness to pray for media members and to pass out New Testaments and grief materials. Chris referred me to a number of people.

This was a unique visit with so many opportunities. I felt the Lord was with me through the whole trip and led me to be able to talk personally with many individuals who asked if we would be willing, with no political agenda, to minister to Jewish, international, and Palestinian press representatives. I said yes. I would be open to reaching out to all the media there. We do not have a point of view politically. Our purpose is to be there for personal support and spiritual encouragement. We would be supportive of an international press in the country.

I went to Ramallah, which is a Palestinian city, to meet with the director of the BBC Media Action group. I met the director, who is Palestinian and was born in Ramallah. He has traveled to several countries because of his work. He is a very kind, patient, attentive host. He was trying to figure out who we were and what we would do in Ramallah. Because of his experiences, he believed we could be of help, especially in Gaza. The director said that all those I met felt a good vibe from me. Their office would always be open to me, and they would do anything they could to help. This was all so strange to me, because it was the first time I had been in an office of all Palestinians and I was treated so graciously. They were completely open to me as a Christian. They worked for a company that is funded by a nonprofit of the BBC. Their work was to provide help to the media people of this area. I sensed the Lord's presence from beginning to end when we were in Israel. God opened one door after another. As I visited and prayed with people, I became so aware of the stress that they live under. Many are expecting war in the Middle East, not just skirmishes from Hamas. They are aware of the critical role in world history of the place in which they live. There is such a mix in Israel: Jewish, Christian, Muslim, and Palestinian. I was so thankful for the opportunity to minister to them.

In conclusion, I want to leave a word of encouragement with anyone reading this chapter. I was an infant abandoned in a garage. God fostered me through a wonderful Christian home and supernaturally called me at age fifteen to reach the lost for Jesus. I moved by the power of the Holy Spirit outside of the mainstream church, taking the message of Jesus's redemptive love to the fast lane of Hollywood and beyond. God has been faithful to provide for my ministry, which has led a great number of precious, vulnerable people from destruction

Media Fellowship International

in the grasp of the entertainment industry to freedom in salvation through the redeeming blood of Jesus Christ. If I can reach the lost for Jesus, so can you. God needs Christians to reach out and bring others to Jesus before his glorious return.[3]

Resources

Watch Gemma Wenger's interview of Pastor Bob Rieth speaking about the Media Fellowship International meetings in New York City sponsored by Michael P. Grace II on her YouTube show *Beauty For Ashes*: https://www.youtube.com/watch?v=J8b7GYfI_iA.

---

3. DeFazio and Spencer, *Redeeming the Screens*, 152–58.

Left to right: Bob Yerkes, Dorothy Yerkes, Faye Alexander, and Rose Alexander

BOB YERKES

Top Hollywood stuntman Bob Yerkes (February 11, 1932–October 1, 2024) was a director of Pastor Bob Rieth's Media Fellowship International.

Bob's chapter in *Redeeming the Screens*, "Hollywood's *Circus of the Stars* Stuntman," details his involvement in the formative years of MFI:

> I first became involved with Media Fellowship International in the 1970s,[1] and am currently a director of MFI. At that time, Reverend Bob Rieth, MFI's founder, hosted events at the Marina City Club, often emceed by the multitalented Susan Stafford, former hostess for Merv Griffin's *Wheel of Fortune*. I also met philanthropist Michael P. Grace II at Reverend Rieth's MFI 1980s Bible studies in his Playa del Rey home. I also attended Michael P. Grace

---

1. Clarification: In *Redeeming the Screens*, Bob Yerkes recalled his involvement in the formative years of Pastor Bob's ministry in Hollywood. In the 1970s, Bob Rieth actually teamed up with Johnny Probst at FCAME and had not yet founded MFI. Pastor Bob hosted FCAME's high-profile luncheons at the Marina City Club, moderated by Susan Stafford, in the 1970s.

II's World Alliance for Peace Hollywood outreaches in the 1980s and 1990s, hosted by Reverend Bob Rieth and MFI.[2]

Currently, I attend a Bible study at CBS Radford Studios in North Hollywood pastored by Reverend Robert Rieth of Media Fellowship International. In 1955, this was the home of GE Theatre. I recall rigging trapeze at an early GE Theatre program, narrated by Ronald Reagan, about a famous clown played by actor Henry Fonda.[3]

Today, I minister with MFI's national and international outreach to the media during crises. I traveled with MFI on location to Virginia for outreach to the media during the Virginia Tech massacre, to New Orleans for MFI's Hurricane Katrina outreach to the media, and to Israel for MFI's outreach to the media during recent terrorist attacks.

My motivation for ministry to the media could be summed up like this: I was mentored by the world's greatest stuntman who specialized in high work. His name was Jesus Christ. He stood in for everyone up on the cross. And he sustains me by his Spirit.[4]

Bob Yerkes shared his Christian testimony in *Redeeming the Screens*:

> While with Ringling Brothers Circus, I decided to read the Bible. I grew up with a blind Christian aunt who possessed great spiritual insight, and her belief in Jesus impacted my early life, though I was reared in an unbelieving home. As a young adult, I have to confess I read the Bible planning to denounce the truth of it, but I realized that it had to be inspired by God. Steve Terrell, the oldest son in the television series *Life with Father*, took me to the Village Church in Burbank, California. At twenty-five years old, I became a believer. I formed a group at Ringling Brothers Circus to read and study the Bible. I got my

2. DeFazio and Spencer, *Redeeming the Screens*, 60–61.
3. DeFazio and Spencer, *Redeeming the Screens*, 58.
4. DeFazio and Spencer, *Redeeming the Screens*, 61.

two friends, Reggie Armour and Bill Snyder, interested, and the first Bible study meeting was held in Little Rock, Arkansas. The group was nondenominational, including Roman Catholics as well as Protestants. My pastor, Reverend Phil Gibson, sent literature to help us in our worship.[5]

Throughout his career as a circus acrobat and through his legendary work as one of Hollywood's top stuntmen, as the Spirit of God brought him through various stunt accidents, he heard the Lord impress into his heart a Bible verse, Zech 4:6 (KJV): "This is the word of the Lord unto Zerubbabel, saying, Not by might nor by power, but by my spirit." The purpose of this message from God to Zechariah was to encourage Joshua and Zerubbabel in their work of restoring the temple and the nation of Judah after the Babylonian captivity. They were shown that the true source of power was not merely by might, not by human power, but by the Holy Spirit's anointing. This vision assured Israel that, despite the hindrance of the work on the temple, Zerubbabel would finish it (Zech 4:8–10). Bob credits his spiritual and physical survival to his understanding of his vision to Zechariah: not by force, nor by strength, but by my Spirit. . . . Bob realizes that these keywords were highlighted for him by God's Spirit. Bob has come to realize that it is only through God's spirit that he has come to accomplish anything of true value. Zechariah 4:6 reminds Bob continually that he is on Jesus' side, and Bob has brought that message to many. . . . As he lived for God, Bob was determined not to trust only in his own strength or abilities but rather to depend on God. Bob has moved in the power of the Holy Spirit, becoming a well known witness for Jesus in the acrobatic stunt and entertainment industry. Bob Yerkes credits his spiritual and physical survival to his understanding of God's vision to Zechariah.[6]

---

5. DeFazio and Spencer, *Redeeming the Screens*, 57.

6. DeFazio and Spencer, *Redeeming the Screens*, 54–55, reprinted with Bob Yerkes's permission in DeFazio, *Commission*, 44.

Media Fellowship International

Editorial note: I am grateful that Bob Yerkes contributed to *Creative Ways to Build Christian Community, Redeeming the Screens, The Commission,* and *The Journey Home* so that I am able to quote him in this book. I will never forget the time he took me to a circus tent and stopped to share his faith with a trapeze artist. His heart was so great to reach the lost for Jesus.

In Pastor Bob's words:

> In the same way that Philip ran alongside a chariot to ask the Ethiopian if he understood a passage from Scripture, the MFI chaplain team follows the Spirit's leading, coming alongside people in the entertainment industry who are in need.[7]

The New York Times eulogized Bob Yerkes as a legend in the circus and stunt world and a devout Christian.[8] Members like Bob Yerkes made MFI a model outreach to the entertainment world.

Resources

Watch Bob Yerkes read his contribution to *The Commission*: https://www.youtube.com/watch?v=HmJKCU4ezEM.

---

7. DeFazio and Spencer, *Redeeming the Screens*, 158.
8. Rosenwald, "Bob Yerkes."

Charlene Eber

CHARLENE EBER

I am happy to participate in this tribute to Pastor Bob Rieth. I recall Reverend Bob Rieth's dedication to Michael P. Grace II's World Alliance For Peace outreaches in New York City. Pastor Bob and MFI hosted Mr. Grace's quarterly high-profile testimonial luncheons in New York City and he faithfully taught Scripture and prayed for the homeless who attended Mr. Grace's monthly McDonald's restaurant outreach in NYC. I praised Pastor Bob in *Creative Ways to Build Christian Community* for feeding the rich and the rundown of New York City the word of God.[1]

Pastor Robert Rieth, of Media Fellowship International, faithfully took time from his own ministerial responsibilities to encourage those who attended the meetings with insights from Scripture.[2]

1. Charlene Eber, interview with Jeanne DeFazio by text, Oct. 24, 2024.
2. DeFazio and Lathrop, *Creative Ways*, 3.

Media Fellowship International

In the early 1990s, Pastor Robert Rieth's Media Fellowship International hosted The New York City high-profile Christian Testimonial Luncheons which were sponsored by World Alliance for Peace. These events were held quarterly at prominent New York locations, including Sardi's Restaurant, Mickey Mantle's Restaurant, the Armory, and the Soldiers, Sailors, and Airmen's Club. Guests heard powerful Christian testimonies from baseball legend Bobby Richardson; Chaplain Susan Stafford, PhD, best known as the original *Wheel of Fortune* hostess who was a young pioneer for women in game shows and is today a humanitarian; J. J. Ebaugh of CNN; Governor of Missouri, John Ashcroft (who later became the US Attorney General); and international songstress Martha Reyes.[3]

Michael P. Grace II[4]

3. DeFazio and Lathrop, *Creative Ways*, 10.

4. Winston Grace gave permission for this photo of his father to be published in this book. Interview with Jeanne DeFazio by email, Nov. 27, 2024.

Charlene Eber

These meetings were sponsored by the World Alliance for Peace. Charlene Eber, secretary and director of advertising for WAFP, explains:

> I had the privilege to volunteer as secretary and director of advertising for fourteen years with World Alliance for Peace. The inspiration for it was a phenomenal experience. A voice in the night woke me with a message, part of which was, "We are the children. We are the world. This world does not belong to us. It belongs to our children and our children's children. We are merely caretakers of the future. We need to start making a difference now." I shared this with Michael Grace the next day, and his response was that we have to do something with it. Together, we came up with the name, World Alliance for Peace. He brought the idea to Archbishop Metropolitan John Stanley, founder of the Orthodox Church of the East. Our vision was that the whole world is our community, as we are all God's children and we are all responsible for each other.[5]

Charlene Eber shared her testimony in *Redeeming the Screens*:

> In the early 1980s, veteran actress Joan Caulfield found an advertisement for Video Ventures in the Los Angeles telephone book. She contacted Hollywood director and producer Charlene Eber from that advertisement at the request of her longtime friend, Michael P. Grace II. Mr. Grace, a former Broadway producer and the chief executive officer of Grace Motion Pictures, asked Charlene to film a ministry event for Breath of the Spirit, the international Christian ministry of Michelle Corral and her mother, Joanne Petronella. Charlene's husband, Ken, asked Joanne to pray for Charlene, who was dying of cancer. One night, Charlene had a life-changing experience. She knew at that moment that Jesus had healed her. After her medical reports evidenced the miraculous recovery, Charlene recalls walking through the University of Southern California (USC) Hospital wondering why people in the hallway were applauding. She thought

---

5. DeFazio and Lathrop, *Creative Ways*, 2.

perhaps there was a Hollywood movie star passing by, and then she realized that the staff was cheering for her for a miraculous recovery that defied the understanding of modern science and medicine.

Charlene grew up in a Roman Catholic home where she knew and loved Jesus, but her life-changing and miraculous healing from terminal cancer gave her relationship with Jesus a new start. Her personal experience of Jesus's healing touch allowed her to understand at the depths of her heart and soul the extent of God's mercy and love. Her answered prayer opened up a way for her to live her life more completely for Jesus.[6]

Pastor Bob Rieth's meetings impacted my spiritual life. His teaching from Scripture encouraged me as I juggled marriage, motherhood, and the responsibilities of running a production company in Hollywood. Psalm 133:1 (KJV) declares: "Behold, how good and how pleasant it is for brethren to dwell together in unity!" I looked forward to MFI meetings with my Christian colleagues in the industry. Together we praised and thanked God in worship and prayer. We shared food and fellowship and had fun together. Thank you Pastor Bob.[7]

Resources

Watch Charlene Eber speak about her work with Michael P. Grace II and World Alliance for Peace in the promo for the book *Creative Ways to Build Christian Community*, with Susan Stafford and Jeanne DeFazio: https://www.youtube.com/watch?v=9KJ_lIbpi_Y.

---

6. DeFazio and Spencer, *Redeeming the Screens*, 128.
7. Charlene Eber, interview with Jeanne DeFazio by text, Oct. 24, 2024.

Those Who Attended Media
Fellowship International Events
Honor Pastor Bob Rieth

Billie Hemphill[1]

BILLIE HEMPHILL

In 2016, I visited Los Angeles. A mutual friend of Bob Yerkes and mine suggested that Bob might let me stay during my visit in his famous Clown Trailer. Bob Yerkes very kindly allowed me to stay and return on my visits to Los Angeles from my home in Oregon. It was very gracious of him. Bob Yerkes had undergone cataract surgery, but his night vision prevented him from driving to evening prayer meetings. Bob would always ask me to drive him when he was no longer able to drive. I drove him to Billy Davis Jr. and Marilyn McCoo's Christian outreaches as well, and to CBS Studios where MFI Pastor Bob Rieth would often meet with former CBS executive Charles Cappleman, among others. At these meetings Pastor Bob would teach from Scripture and pray with and for anyone who shared a prayer request.

As Julia C. Davis explained in the foreword of this book, Pastor Bob was a great relational evangelist. He listened from the heart and encouraged everyone who attended his meetings. When Pastor Bob Rieth passed in 2022, it was a great loss for many MFI members. Bob

---

1. Jeanne DeFazio gave permission for this photo to be published in this book, Nov. 30, 2024.

Media Fellowship International

Yerkes and Pastor Bob were very close and Bob Yerkes felt the loss deeply. Jeanne DeFazio stayed in the Clown Trailer in Bob Yerkes's backyard while writing the Media Fellowship International chapter that begins this book.[2] Jeanne told me that Bob's wife Marion, who died in 2018, helped Pastor Bob organize that chapter and Jeanne formatted it for publication. The chapter was published originally in *Redeeming the Screens*, a book edited by Jeanne DeFazio and William David Spencer. *Redeeming the Screens* contains testimonies from Christians who were MFI members and attendees of MFI events. I mention all of this to demonstrate how deeply interconnected MFI members were with Pastor Bob and each other.

Julia C. Davis also cites Acts 17:26–28 (NKJV) in the foreword of this book: "And He has made from one blood every nation of men to dwell on all the face of the earth, and has determined their preappointed times and the boundaries of their dwellings, so that they should seek the Lord, in the hope that they might grope for Him and find Him, though He is not far from each one of us; for in Him we live and move and have our being, as also some of your own poets have said, 'For we are also His offspring.'"

What I loved about Pastor Bob was that he created an atmosphere in MFI where Jesus's love embraced us. The power of the Holy Spirit gathered us together under Pastor Bob's anointing, so that we were brothers and sisters in the Lord despite differences. I bonded with those who attended because I felt the love of Jesus from Pastor Bob and in fellowship with my Christian brothers and sisters. I shared these memories because Pastor Bob Rieth and Media Fellowship International were a great blessing in my life.[3]

---

2. Jeanne DeFazio organized the MFI events in Los Angeles and in New York City from 1983 to 1995.

3. Billie Hemphill, interview with Jeanne DeFazio by text, Oct. 24, 2024.

Yvonnette O'Neal

YVONNETTE O'NEAL

I was honored to meet Pastor Bob Rieth at an MFI luncheon at the Waldorf Hotel in Washington, DC. Jeanne DeFazio invited me and my dear friend and colleague Julia C. Davis to the luncheon. Julia authored the foreword of this book. Julia and I both sensed the presence of God in Pastor Bob when he prayed over the distinguished guests who attended. I spoke briefly after the luncheon with Pastor Bob and shared details about my ministry, Ambassadors Prayer Network. Pastor Bob took the time to encourage me in my ministry. This was long before I became a visiting chaplain at the United Nations. When the editor of this project, Jeanne DeFazio, asked me to contribute, I thought back to the conversation with Pastor Bob and decided to contribute to thank him for his encouragement.

Media Fellowship International

Encouragement, as *Circus of the Stars*'s Bob Yerkes explains, is one of Pastor Bob's great gifts: "Pastor Bob Rieth is down to earth and kind. He listens and encourages us, sharing Scripture, praying with us and for us. Under his pastoral anointing, we bond and feel great joy in Christian community devoted to bringing others to Jesus."[1]

As an evangelist, I recognize Pastor Bob and MFI broke through cultural barriers. Culturally diverse brothers and sisters accomplished the Great Commission under his leadership. Media Fellowship International was ahead of its time in that respect. Pastor Rieth and MFI fostered inclusion and their work fit into the larger movement toward a truly equitable multiracial America.

In Matt 28:18–20 (NIV) Jesus instructs his disciples: "Then Jesus came to them and said, 'All authority in heaven and on earth has been given to me. Therefore go and make disciples of all nations, baptizing them in the name of the Father and of the Son and of the Holy Spirit, and teaching them to obey everything I have commanded you. And surely I am with you always, to the very end of the age.'" "God is no respecter of persons" (Acts 10:34 KJV). He brings all Christians together to gather the lost just like Pastor Bob did in Media Fellowship International.[2]

Resources

Yvonnette welcomes anyone who needs prayer to call on Fridays at 9:00 p.m. (EST). Dial 1-872-240-3412 and enter access code 332-85-709#.

Watch Yvonnette O'Neal speak about her ministry at the Gordon-Conwell Theological Seminary's Boston

1. Bob Yerkes, interview by telephone with author, July 2012. DeFazio and Lathrop, *Creative Ways*, 8.

2. Yvonnette O'Neal gave permission for this photo to be published in this book along with her interview with Jeanne DeFazio by text, Oct. 23, 2024.

Those Who Attended Media Fellowship International Events

Campus for Urban Ministerial Education Chapel "Creative Ways to Build Christian Community": https://www.youtube.com/watch?v=WKRN_XAvwHU.

Martha Reyes and Mother Teresa

MARTHA REYES

Martha Reyes was born in Puerto Rico and has resided in California, ministering to Hispanics in the United States and internationally, since 1978. She has traveled to more than twenty-two Latin American countries and many parts of Europe and the Middle East giving concerts and retreats on inner healing and participating as a guest speaker in national and international conventions on healing and restoration. From 1992 until the year 2000, she organized the acclaimed Hosanna multifestival conventions, international events with representatives from thirty countries in music, theatre, and the arts, held annually in Mexico, Florida, and Israel. Martha is the author of *Jesús y la Mujer Herida* (*Jesus and the Wounded Woman*) and *Jesucristo, Tu Psicólogo Personal* (*Jesus is Your Own Personal Psychologist*). She has also written articles for a number of Spanish-language publications.[1]

---

1. DeFazio and Spencer, *Redeeming the Screens*, 90–91.

I am happy to participate in this tribute to Pastor Bob Rieth. The last time I had the opportunity to see him was at Bee Beyer's home in Bel Air about ten years ago. Bee's daughter, Gemma Wenger, was filming her television show *Beauty For Ashes*. Pastor Bob and I were both being interviewed by Gemma. Bob warmly greeted me and let me know how much he appreciated my performance and testimony at an MFI NYC luncheon in the early 1990s. I have performed and testified in many high-profile and distinguished venues but I am grateful to God that Pastor Bob and Michael P. Grace II brought me to New York to speak and perform for MFI. Romans 12:5 describes the MFI experience exactly: "So we, being many, are one body in Christ, and every one members one of another" (KJV). Pastor Bob made you feel like you were one of the family at MFI, and that he loved you and Jesus loved you more."[2]

Resources

Watch Gemma Wenger's interview of Martha Reyes, founder of Hosanna Foundation, where she speaks about Media Fellowship International's New York City meetings sponsored by Michael P. Grace II on Gemma's YouTube show *Beauty For Ashes*": https://www.youtube.com/watch?v=QoDUN4cTrbo.

---

2. Martha Reyes, interview with Jeanne DeFazio by email, Oct. 25, 2024.

Left to right: Dale Evans, April Shenandoah, and Roy Rogers

April Shenandoah fondly recalls Reverend Bob Rieth pastoring Michael P. Grace II's World Alliance For Peace outreaches in Los Angeles and New York:

> Mr. Grace's dear friend, actress, author, and political activist, April Shenandoah, puts it perfectly: Show business was my God until I met God!
>
> During those years in Hollywood and New York, I attended several Media Fellowship International meetings conducted by Michael Grace. Being a new Christian, I soaked up more godly wisdom at those gatherings than I was aware of at the time. Michael Grace was born with just the right name. He offered "grace" to "all." His ministry to the homeless was heartfelt, as I had the pleasure of experiencing firsthand in Manhattan—upstairs at a McDonald's restaurant. Thank God for the vision that Michael Grace had for others.[1]

April Shenandoah describes a powerful move of the Holy Spirit through the teaching of the word in one of those meetings: During one evening at a McDonald's meeting, a small elderly man stood up to share. I do not know if

---

1. DeFazio and Lathrop, *Creative Ways*, 8–9.

he was homeless or just down on his luck, but I do know that I will never forget him. As he reached into his pocket and pulled out a small Bible, he spoke words filled with faith and such conviction that my spirit leaped for joy. His soft-spoken passion raised my faith when he told us not to look to people for anything, but to trust God for every need. This man was rich in my eyes. That is what these meetings were all about: being inspired and led by the Holy Spirit.[2]

MFI members lived Paul's vision described in 1 Cor 12:25 (NIV): "So that there should be no division in the body, but that its parts should have equal concern for each other."[3]

Resources

Watch Gemma Wenger's interview of April Shenandoah where she speaks about Media Fellowship International and her chapter in *Redeeming the Screens* on Gemma's YouTube show *Beauty For Ashes*": https://www.youtube.com/watch?v=vi7_aqKbOsM.

---

2. DeFazio and Spencer, *Redeeming the Screens*, 101–2. Spencer and Spencer, *Christian Egalitarian Leadership*, 122.

3. April Shenandoah, interview with Jeanne DeFazio by phone, Dec. 19, 2024.

Aaron Ezra Mann and Susan Stafford

Academy Award-winning producer Aaron Mann (aka Ezra Mann) was reared in an Orthodox Jewish tradition. His parents were Holocaust survivors. He is acknowledged in *Berkeley Street Theatre* for making a courageous paradigm cultural shift in the Hollywood community by accepting Jesus as Messiah, Lord, and Savior. His powerful play *Otto and the White Dove* is an autobiographical account of his conversion. In it, the White Dove (a manifestation of the Holy Spirit) expounds the word of God and brings Otto, a Holocaust survivor, to Jesus.

Aaron identifies his life-changing experience as he broke orthodox Hebrew tradition through the power of the Holy Spirit to encounter the risen Jesus in Hollywood's evangelistic Christian communities. Along with Susan Stafford, Patti Zuckor, Gavin and Patti MacLeod, LeaAnn Pendergrass, and Linda Chapman, Aaron prays for and ministers God's word to Jewish and gentile members of the entertainment industry.[1]

I am grateful for the opportunity to contribute to this project and pay tribute to our beloved Pastor Bob Rieth. As a convert to Christianity from a Jewish background, I felt at home at Media Fellowship International meetings because Messianic Jews in the industry like Al Kasha, Peter Engel, and Joe Glaiberg attended. Pastor Bob's pastoral anointing enabled him to reach the up and out and the down and out for Jesus. It wasn't unusual for an industry heavy hitter to sit next to a struggling actor at

---

1. Spencer and Spencer, *Christian Egalitarian Leadership*, 124.

Those Who Attended Media Fellowship International Events

MFI luncheons. Bob would often graciously host those who couldn't afford the cost of the meal who needed to hear the word of God and have loving Christian fellowship. MFI lived out the Acts 2:42 (NIV) narrative: "They devoted themselves to the apostles' teaching and to fellowship, to the breaking of bread and to prayer."[2]

Resources

Watch Susan Stafford interview Aaron Ezra Mann on her YouTube show *Out of the Box*: https://www.youtube.com/watch?v=yhUNhi_xmBw.

---

2. Aaron Ezra Mann gave permission for this photo to be published in this book along with the interview with Jeanne DeFazio by email, Oct. 25, 2024.

Gemma Wenger

GEMMA WENGER

Gemma Wenger is a Christian pastor, interview show producer/host, singer/songwriter, and author. She is the producer/host for *Gemma Wenger's Hollywood* and *Beauty for Ashes*, which were official selections in the 2021 International Christian Film and Music Festival. She is the songwriter for "Trust" as well having been a contributing author to multiple books.[1]

I am honored to participate in this tribute to Pastor Bob Rieth and Media Fellowship International. In my formative years, my mother, Bee Beyer, and I attended Pastor Bob's Los Angeles MFI prayer meetings and luncheons sponsored by Michael P. Grace II.[2]

Beulah Bee Beyer Wenger, editor of the *Hollywood Times*, and her daughter Gemma, producer of the international television series *Gemma Wenger's Hollywood* and *Beauty for Ashes*, brought members of the entertainment industry to the event. Beulah Bee Beyer Wenger remembers Mr. Grace: "As in biblical times, many were named according to their character; Michael Grace was also

---

1. Wikipedia, "Gemma Wenger," para. 1.
2. Gemma Wenger, interview with Jeanne DeFazio by text, Oct. 26, 2024.

appropriately named because he was constantly helping people to become Christians and to lead them to God's amazing grace."[3]

Gemma Wenger recalls Mr. Grace's influence upon her a young child:
As a young child, I remember Mr. Grace gathering people together in churches, restaurants, and homes to hear and grow in the word of God. He was a pioneer in bringing the gifts of the Spirit to people who were hungry for a deeper walk with the Lord. The seeds that were planted in my heart through Mr. Grace's outreach have resulted in me starting my own evangelical and prophetic international ministry. Mr. Grace was a friend, a leader, and a spiritual guide to a body of people called by God. He truly was raised up for a specific time and a purpose to break the bonds of religious tradition and usher in a new era of God's anointing.[4]

Media Fellowship International was a manifestation of the Trinitarian blessing of Paul the apostle in 2 Cor 13:14 (NIV). Pastor Bob began MFI meetings with prayer: "May the grace of the Lord Jesus Christ, and the love of God, and the fellowship of the Holy Spirit be with you all." Grace, love, and fellowship with one another came from God in Christ through the Spirit to us all.[5]

Resources

Watch Gemma Wenger's interview with Jeanne DeFazio where she speaks about her work for Media Fellowship International sponsored by Michael P. Grace II on Gemma's YouTube show *Beauty for Ashes*: https://www.youtube.com/watch?v=78JbTZEzZc8.

3. Bee Beyer, interview by email, July 2012. DeFazio and Lathrop, *Creative Ways*, 4.

4. Gemma Wenger, interview by email July 2012. DeFazio and Lathrop, *Creative Ways*, 4–5.

5. Gemma Wenger, interview with Jeanne DeFazio by text, Oct. 26, 2024.

Wally Bruder

WALLY BRUDER

It is a great honor to be included in this tribute to Pastor Bob Rieth and Media Fellowship International. I regularly attended the monthly MFI Bible studies that were sponsored by Michael P. Grace II during the 1980s and 1990s. My area of specialty as a regular participant was to make sure everyone in the group got a hug. Pastor Bob and Mr. Grace often remarked with a smile that I broke the ice at the beginning of the meetings by embracing the guests. I was not a high-profile, glamorous attendee. I embraced everyone regardless of culture, gender, or economic status. When the presence of God fell over the room, after praise and worship and Pastor Bob's teaching, the Spirit of the living God was there to embrace us all. Hebrews 10:24–25 (ESV) describes MFI fellowship: "And let us consider how to stir up one another to love and good works, not neglecting to meet together, as is the habit of some, but encouraging one another, and all the more as you see the Day drawing near."[1]

Those who were weary in spirit found solace in Pastor Rieth's teaching and the encouragement of the worship. One person who was especially faithful to the monthly meeting was Wally Bruder. Wally shared Jesus's love by hugging everyone who attended and by faithfully praying for their concerns. In his own words, "It was a privilege and joy being part of this group where together we were encouraged and richly blessed in pursuing the priceless treasure of being drawn deep into the heart of Jesus, first for our own edification, and out of the overflow we freely shared Jesus's transforming love, joy, peace, and presence with everyone else.[2]

RESOURCES

Listen to Wally Bruder's testimony: https://www.youtube.com/watch?v=T0OrETV61TE.

1. Wally Bruder gave permission for this photo to be published in this book along with the interview with Jeanne DeFazio by email, Oct. 26, 2024.

2. Wally Bruder, interview by email, August 2012. DeFazio and Lathrop, *Creative Ways*, 4.

Left to right: Rod Jackson, Joanne Cash Yates, Kimberly Jackson, and Sheri Pedigo at the Cowboy Church in Nashville, Tennessee

SHERI PEDIGO

Triple-Platinum songwriter and director Sheri Pedigo grew up in a small town in Kentucky. At the early age of eight she was singing and writing songs on piano. She's had success in many facets of the music business as a hit songwriter, the owner and operator of her own publishing company, and as a recording and performing artist herself. She has shared the stage with numerous artists of note and is also a contributing author to the book *Redeeming the Screens*. As a filmmaker, her creative vision began when she wrote the song "Father Me." This song is a major inspiration for the documentary and becomes the film's soundtrack as the audience moves through a journey of discovery and healing.

Redeeming the Screens: Living Stories of Media "Ministers" Bringing the Message of Jesus Christ to the Entertainment Industry offers testimonies from world-class relational media evangelists telling their own stories of

Those Who Attended Media Fellowship International Events

what brought them to receive Jesus and how the power of his death and resurrection on the cross helped them through the challenges in their lives.

Sheri Pedigo's chapter, "Flight of the Butterfly," is an honest testimonial that started with a young girl's vision to one day having her voice heard throughout the world proclaiming the power of God's love through music and words.[1]

It is an honor to participate in this tribute to Pastor Bob Rieth. Jeanne DeFazio, the editor of this book, texted me and asked me to describe the impact of Pastor Bob and Media Fellowship International on my life. Over the years I attended MFI prayer meetings in restaurants, at CBS Radford Studio in North Hollywood, and the Annual MFI Breakfast at The Beverly Hills Hotel. At those meetings, Pastor Bob was always supportive and encouraging. He prayed for me. He knew my heart to proclaim the power of God's love through music and words.

Since first meeting with Pastor Bob, my song "Father Me" has received accolades in the music industry and is the soundtrack for my award-winning documentary, "Father Me." The line in that song that stands out in my mind right now is, "He took the nail out of my heart and put it in His hand." I share these lyrics today because they represent the power of Jesus's redemptive love.

When a shepherd of lost sheep like Pastor Bob passes you realize the extent of his calling. He shared God's love and brought us together to worship. He taught us the word and when the Spirit of God fell on his meetings, we prayed together.

MFI modeled 1 John 1:6–7 (ESV): "If we say we have fellowship with him while we walk in darkness, we lie and do not practice the truth. But if we walk in the light, as he is in the light, we have fellowship with one another, and the blood of Jesus his Son cleanses us from all sin." Under Pastor Bob's anointing, hurting people in the industry were healed and set free because they received Jesus as Lord and Savior, repented of sin, and accepted God's

1. Stage 32, "Sheri Pedigo."

forgiveness and loving embrace. To paraphrase "Father Me," Jesus took the nail out of their hearts and put it in His hand.[2]

Resources

Listen to Sheri Pedigo read her contribution to *The Commission*: https://www.youtube.com/watch?v=n_hSa2JhgLw.

---

2. Sheri Pedigo, interview with Jeanne DeFazio by text, Oct. 28, 2024.

Left to right: Advisory Board member and Academy-Award-winning composer Al Kasha, Bob Rieth, and recording artist Donna Summer

Who we are: Media Fellowship International (MFI) is a Christian ministry that works primarily with leaders in the professional entertainment and media industries. MFI provides a peer group atmosphere in which members can confidentially share their concerns and experiences, talk about Christ, pray with each other, and study the Bible together.[1]

---

1. Thanks to Carolyn Ridley, founding board member of the National Advisory Board of Media Fellowship International, for permission to include this photo and explanation of the mission of MFI from an undated MFI brochure. Interview with Jeanne DeFazio by email, Nov. 26, 2024.

MFI Executive Director Bob Rieth and National Advisory Board member and syndicated columnist Cal Thomas, The National Prayer Breakfast

Annual MFI Outreach Luncheon at the National Press Club in Washington, DC

National activities: Each year MFI has the opportunity to select the media delegation to attend The Annual National Prayer Breakfast in Washington, DC, hosted by our President and members of Congress. MFI hosts two days of activities in conjunction with this national event

Those Who Attended Media Fellowship International Events

for the purpose of building and encouraging relationships. A much smaller MFI delegation is also invited to travel to London and participate in their National Prayer Breakfast.[1]

Cal Thomas: "Pastor Bob Rieth invited guests to a dinner I hosted as part of The National Breakfast events for thirty years."[2]

---

1. Thanks to Carolyn Ridley, founding board member of the National Advisory Board of Media Fellowship International, for permission to include these photos and the description of MFI's national activities from an undated MFI brochure. Interview with Jeanne DeFazio by email, Nov. 26, 2024.

2. Cal Thomas, interview with Jeanne DeFazio by email, Nov. 25, 2024.

MFI Executive Director Bob Rieth presents the
MFI *Ambassador Award* to Peter Engel

MEDIA FELLOWSHIP INTERNATIONAL'S *AMBASSADOR AWARD*

Advisory Board member Peter Engel was the recipient of MFI's 1996 *Ambassador Award*. Peter is the executive producer of five current television programs including *Saved By The Bell* and *California Dreams*.[1]

---

1. Thanks to Carolyn Ridley, founding board member of the National Advisory Board of Media Fellowship International, for permission to include this photo and excerpt from MFI's newsletter, *On Location* (Spring 1997) 6. Interview with Jeanne DeFazio by email, Nov. 26, 2024.

Left to right: Bob Rieth, Howard Wolf, Billy Davis Jr., and Marilyn McCoo

MEDIA FELLOWSHIP INTERNATIONAL'S TENTH ANNIVERSARY

Tenth Anniversary Celebration . . . In the beginning: The evening opened with a concert by the dynamic husband and wife music duo, Billy Davis Jr. and Marilyn McCoo, who have been involved since the first meeting of MFI back in 1987. Shown here with Bob Rieth and Howard Wolf.[1]

---

1. Thanks to Carolyn Ridley, founding board member of the National Advisory Board of Media Fellowship International, for permission to publish this photo and description of MFI's Tenth Anniversary Event from MFI's newsletter, *On Location* (Fall 1997) 3. Interview with Jeanne DeFazio by email, Nov. 26, 2024.

MFI goes to Israel (left to right): Paul Rieth, Susan Stafford, Kate MacMurray, June Havers MacMurray, and Bob Rieth[1]

MEDIA FELLOWSHIP INTERNATIONAL ISRAEL TOURS

Media Fellowship International (MFI) and Pastor Bob Rieth are taking a small group June 1st to June 11th, 2020. (June 13th if you'd like to add Petra). We will visit Nazareth, Jerusalem, Galilee, Masada, the Garden of Gethsemane, Bethlehem, the Old City, and more. We will also have the opportunity to take a boat ride in the Sea of Galilee, walk beside the River Jordan and be baptized, and stand before the Western Wall (Wailing Wall). If time allows, you'll have the chance to swim in the Dead Sea. In following days, we will walk in the Old City, then travel to Mount Zion and go to the Upper Room. From there it's on to the Tomb of King David and the Garden Tomb.

MFI and Pastor Bob have had the opportunity to take about ten small groups over the years. Pastor Bob has also been there himself, for specific pastoral and ministry purposes, another three or four times. It is a place that calls to him. He would be honored to be able to share his love for this country and its history with you.[2]

1. Thanks to Carolyn Ridley, founding board member of the National Advisory Board of Media Fellowship International, for permission to publish this photo from an undated MFI brochure. Interview with Jeanne DeFazio by email, Nov. 26, 2024.

2. Media Fellowship International website https://mediafellowship.org/.

Pat Boone and Susan Stafford, Media Fellowship's 23rd Praise Brunch and Celebration of Life for Pastor Bob Rieth, April 15, 2023[1]

Pastor Bob Rieth touched the lives of every contributing author to this book.

> He had a way with people that let each person he came in contact with know that they truly mattered. What a gift! Bob had a gift of faith and was a visionary in prayerful planning. No matter what, the things that always came first were the Lord and his desire to share His saving grace with others, and his beloved family.[2]

---

1. Many thanks to Gemma Wenger for permission to publish this photo, interview with Jeanne DeFazio by text, Nov. 27, 2024.

2. *Valley City Times Record*, "Pastor Robert Rieth."

Conclusion

Susan Stafford

SUSAN STAFFORD

This conclusion tells the story of Media Fellowship International in images that evoke precious memories of a family of believers living out their faith in a supportive, loving, and encouraging way. I chose to contribute to this book because, as Pastor Bob explains:

> The celebrity Christian testimony is a key strategy of MFI's practical theology. People can argue theology, but they cannot argue with a testimony, because our stories are what they are.[1]

My celebrity testimony is included in Jeanne DeFazio's chapter, "The Multicultural Aspect of Egalitarian Leadership," in Spencer and Spencer's book, *Christian Egalitarian Leadership*:

> One of the most powerful witnesses to the move of the Holy Spirit recorded in *Redeeming the Screens* is the testimony of Susan Stafford, [original] *Wheel of Fortune* hostess. Susan had achieved major success and fame in

---

1. DeFazio and Spencer, *Redeeming the Screens*, 155.

Hollywood. After a divorce and her disenchantment with *Wheel of Fortune* after her co-host Chuck Woolery left the program, Susan experienced a great void in her life. She describes visiting India with Father Herbert DeSouza and ministering with Mother Teresa among the lepers and the dying as an experience that revived her spiritually and renewed her sense of purpose. Susan left *Wheel of Fortune* on October 22, 1982. Her popularity had engaged Susan in a life relating to fans, many of whom wrote her about their battles with cancer. She began ministering to cancer patients at the Dr. John Stehlin Cancer Center in Houston's St. Joseph Hospital in 1982. Subsequently, Susan cared for Rock Hudson during his much-publicized death from AIDS in the mid-1980s. Joining spiritual forces with Pat and Shirley Boone, Gavin and Patti MacLeod, and Father Terry Sweeney, Susan brought the word of God to Rock Hudson in a critical moment of his life:

> The fear of contagion at Rock Hudson's deathbed was great. Shirley and Pat Boone, Gavin and Patti MacLeod, and I were the only outsiders who came in to minister at Rock's deathbed. We called in Father Terry Sweeney, SJ, because Rock was a Roman Catholic. The loss of Rock as a friend was heartbreaking. I am grateful that Rock came to Jesus on his deathbed, and I have the promise of seeing this beloved friend again in heaven.[2]

Susan's ministry flourished [as she prayed and ministered with prominent Christians] in the entertainment world: Pat and his late wife Shirley Boone, Marilyn McCoo and Billy Davis Jr., Bob Rieth, and Bob Yerkes. She continues reaching out to the sick and dying in the gay community, teaching the word of God through the power of the Holy Spirit.[3]

---

2. DeFazio, "The Multicultural Aspect of Egalitarian Leadership," in Spencer and Spencer, *Christian Egalitarian Leadership*, 121. DeFazio and Spencer, *Redeeming the Screens*, 50.

3. DeFazio, "The Multicultural Aspect of Egalitarian Leadership," in Spencer and Spencer, *Christian Egalitarian Leadership*, 122.

Conclusion

During the 1996 Olympics in Atlanta, MFI brothers and sisters from all over the nation joined Pastor Bob at MFI's Media Support Center to support the US Olympic team and broadcasters of the event.

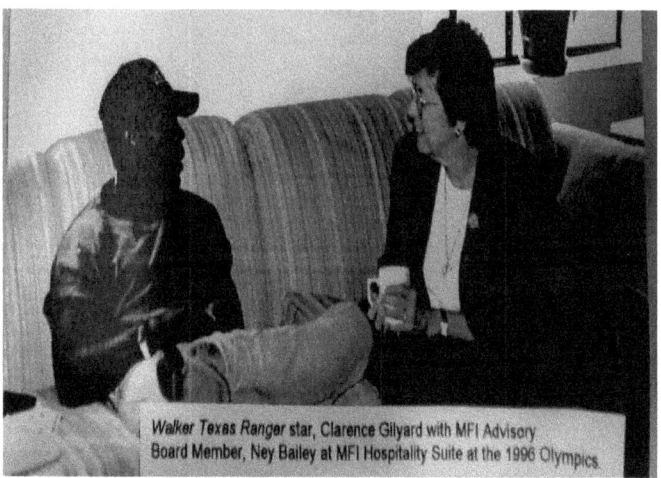

Walker Texas Ranger star Clarence Gilyard with MFI Advisory Board member Ney Bailey at MFI's hospitality suite at the 1996 Olympics[4]

---

4. Thanks to Carolyn Ridley, founding board member of the National Advisory Board of Media Fellowship International, for permission to include this photo from an undated MFI brochure. Interview with Jeanne DeFazio by email, Nov. 26, 2024.

Media Fellowship International

US Olympic Swimmer, Josh Davis, winner of 4 Olympic Gold Medals, shared his testimony at MFI sponsored barbecue in Atlanta during Olympics.

US Olympic swimmer Josh Davis, photographed here with his wife Shantel, is the winner of four Olympic Gold Medals. He shared his testimony at an MFI-sponsored barbecue in Atlanta during the Olympics[5]

The Games were marred by violence on July 27, 1996, when a pipe bomb was detonated at Centennial Olympic Park (which had been built to serve as a public focal point for the festivities), killing two and injuring 111. Years later, Eric Rudolph confessed to the bombing and a series of related terrorist attacks, and was sentenced to life in prison.[6]

---

5. Thanks to Josh Davis for granting permission to publish this photo, interview with Jeanne DeFazio by email, Dec. 22, 2024.
6. Wikipedia, "1996 Summer Olympics," para. 3.

Conclusion

Why did MFI's high-profile Christians unite as a family to support the 1996 US Olympic team and the broadcasters of the event?

MFI's Statement of Faith includes three concepts that explain MFI members' sense of Christian responsibility:

1. The Body: As believers we are all members of Christ's body on earth. We all have the privilege of belonging and the responsibility of participating.
2. The Family: We all believe we are adopted into the Family of God. He is our Father. We are brothers and sisters. It is our opportunity to love, encourage, support, and nourish one another.
3. The Fellowship: As believers [it's important] to be connected to a Christ-centered fellowship. We need the support of one another.[7]

My faith in God and my courage and resolve to continue serving Him in crisis situations grows as I reflect on my MFI family standing in the gap to support the US Olympic team and media broadcasters in the aftermath of a terrorist attack.

Pastor Bob organized nationwide MFI Community Outreach Teams to successfully reach the lost for Jesus:

> MFI is often invited into communities throughout the country to spend a weekend and share the Christian message with youth and adults through schools, community organizations, and churches.[8]

MFI's Statement of Faith follows the scriptural mandate of Paul's Epistle to Titus 3:5–6 (NLT):

> He saved us, not because of the righteous things we had done, but because of his mercy. He washed away our sins,

---

7. Thanks to Carolyn Ridley, founding board member of the National Advisory Board of Media Fellowship International, for permission to publish the MFI Statement of Faith from an undated MFI brochure. Interview with Jeanne DeFazio by email, Nov. 26, 2024.

8. Thanks to Carolyn Ridley, founding board member of the National Advisory Board of Media Fellowship International, for permission to include these excerpts about MFI Community Outreach Teams from an undated MFI brochure. Interview with Jeanne DeFazio by email, Nov. 26, 2024.

giving us a new birth and new life through the Holy Spirit. He generously poured out the Spirit upon us through Jesus Christ our Savior.

We believe that regeneration by the Holy Spirit is absolutely essential for the salvation of lost and sinful men.[9]

Youth come forward for prayer at MFI Youth Outreach in Kansas[10]

Wally Bruder's tribute to Pastor Bob describes his pastoral sensitivity to the Holy Spirit:

> When the presence of God fell over the room after praise and worship and Pastor Bob's teaching, the Spirit of the living God was there to embrace us all. Hebrews 10:24–25 (ESV) describes MFI fellowship: "And let us consider

---

9. Thanks to Carolyn Ridley, founding board member of the National Advisory Board of Media Fellowship International, for permission to include MFI's Statement of Faith from an undated MFI brochure. Interview with Jeanne DeFazio by email, Nov. 26, 2024.

10. Thanks to Carolyn Ridley, founding board member of the National Advisory Board of Media Fellowship International, for permission to include this photo from an undated MFI brochure. Interview with Jeanne DeFazio by email, Nov. 26, 2024.

Conclusion

how to stir up one another to love and good works, not neglecting to meet together, as is the habit of some, but encouraging one another, and all the more as you see the Day drawing near."[11]

I am particularly glad that Wally Bruder quoted Heb 10:24–25. This Scripture speaks of the day of Jesus's imminent return. As precious loved ones go home to be with Jesus like Pastor Bob Rieth, Bob Yerkes, and Chuck Woolery, I feel in my spirit that my focus has to be on Jesus's return so that I prioritize and focus daily on what the Holy Spirit calls me to do.

I am grateful to every contributing author to this book for sharing their memories and photographs to demonstrate Pastor Bob's impact on their lives.

Thanks to African American author and educator Julia C. Davis who explains, in her foreword to this book, why Media Fellowship International is a model Christian outreach to the entertainment industry:

> In first-person accounts, each contributing author demonstrates great love for Pastor Rieth, describing him as a truly remarkable relational evangelist who was a powerful minister of Jesus's redemptive love. Media Fellowship International modeled ways to create Christian community in the media.

Pastor Bob followed the example of Philip in Acts 8:26–35.

> In the same way that Philip ran alongside a chariot to ask the Ethiopian if he understood a passage from Scripture, the MFI chaplain team follows the Spirit's leading, coming alongside people in the entertainment industry who are in need.[12]

---

11. Wally Bruder, interview with Jeanne DeFazio by email, Oct. 26, 2024.
12. DeFazio and Spencer, *Redeeming the Screens*, 158.

Media Fellowship International

MFI Exec. Director Bob Rieth *(left)*, Marion Rieth *(taking picture)* & Carolyn Ridley, from MFI office *(right)* visit *Northern Exposure* as guests of Janine Turner *(2nd from left)* and Kristine Kirsten *(2nd from right)* on location in Roslyn, Washington.

Left to right: Bob Rieth, Janine Turner, Kristine Kirsten, and Carolyn Ridley visit *Northern Exposure* as guests of Janine Turner[13]

13. Thanks to Carolyn Ridley, founding board member of the National Advisory Board of Media Fellowship International, for permission to include this photo from the summer 1994 Media Fellowship International Newsletter. Interview with Jeanne DeFazio by email, Nov. 26, 2024.

Conclusion

Pastor Bob guided us as MFI members. Through his words in this book, God's Spirit is speaking to us now:

> In conclusion, I want to leave a word of encouragement with anyone reading this chapter. I was an infant abandoned in a garage. God fostered me through a wonderful Christian home and supernaturally called me at age fifteen to reach the lost for Jesus. I was moved by the power of the Holy Spirit outside of the mainstream church, taking the message of Jesus's redemptive love to the fast lane of Hollywood and beyond. God has been faithful to provide for my ministry, which has led a great number of precious, vulnerable people from destruction in the grasp of the entertainment industry to freedom in salvation through the redeeming blood of Jesus Christ. If I can reach the lost for Jesus, so can you. God needs Christians to reach out and bring others to Jesus before his glorious return.[14]

---

14. DeFazio and Spencer, *Redeeming the Screens*, 158.

Afterword
WILLIAM DAVID SPENCER

In 1955, the Fellowship of Christians in the Arts, Media, and Entertainment (FCAME) was founded by an ordained Lutheran minister, Eugene R. Bertermann,[1] noted for his service with both *The Lutheran Hour* radio broadcast and the Lutheran Television of the Lutheran Church–Missouri Synod, and then as executive director of the Lutheran Church–Missouri Synod Foundation. Dr. Bertermann went on to serve as president of the board of directors of the National Religious Broadcasters, executive director and board member of the Far East Broadcasting Company, as well as being a member of the American Bible Society Advisory Council, the Advisory Board of Editors of the International Broadcasters Society, the Advisory Committee of Missions Advanced Research and Communication Center, and others.[2] In short, this was one active, high-profile Lutheran minister and a deeply respected Christian broadcaster. By 1973, his contacts were so widespread they included some of the most famous evangelists of his time, including Billy Graham, Bill Bright (founder of Campus Crusade, or CRU today), Carl F. H. Henry (a former journalist who became a renowned evangelical scholar), Jack Wyrtzen (founder of Word of Life Fellowship and youth-oriented camps), celebrated preachers

---

1. Fellowship of Christians, Archives of Wheaton College. See also Eugene R. Bertermann Papers, Concordia Historical Institute.
2. See Eugene R. Bertermann Papers, Archives of Wheaton College.

such as Stephen Olford and George Sweeting,[3] as well as outspoken Christians in politics like Presidents Dwight Eisenhower,[4] Gerald Ford, and Jimmy Carter, and Senator Mark Hatfield. In the early 1970s, Dr. Bertermann was a planner of Key 73. Dubuque's *Telegraph Herald* reported the event as "a nationwide ecumenical project during 1973 with its motto being 'Calling the Continent to Christ.'" The project was the result of a 1967 interdenominational meeting arranged by Carl F. H. Henry, a Baptist theologian and former editor of *Christianity Today*. Five years of planning on a

---

3. George Sweeting's son was one of the pastors in my birth church, Hydewood Park Baptist Church in North Plainfield, New Jersey.

4. President Eisenhower was often photographed on a Sunday faithfully attending church, encouraging many church-lapsed citizens, like my parents, who had recently become Christians, to do so as well. And, just to clear the air about the continuing slanderous rumor that Ike had an affair while serving overseas, Doug Price, who served on President Eisenhower's White House staff and on the Editorial Advisory Board for archiving Eisenhower's papers at Johns Hopkins University, reports, "Kay Summersby's memoir titled *Past Forgetting: My Love Affair with Dwight D. Eisenhower* turned out not to have been written by Summersby who died within a month of signing a contract to write the book. She never even saw the manuscript which was written by a ghostwriter. Sue Sarafian Jehl, Kay's wartime roommate, said the book 'didn't sound at all like Kay.' And Kay's close friend, Anther Saxe, wife of the executor of Summersby's estate, said 'Kay never saw a word of [the book], the whole thing was made up.' . . . When war correspondent and Eisenhower friend Virgil Pinkley asked Sgt. McKeogh, Ike's wartime orderly, about the rumored affair, McKeogh said 'at least a dozen of us made up the Eisenhower household or family overseas' and observed 'if there had been an affair, someone would have seen or learned about it and would have told or written that story for money. You can usually count on one Judas among twelve, but no one ever told a story.' McKeogh also said 'that stuff about an affair with Kay is sheer nonsense. I put the boss to bed every night and there was no one else in bed. In the morning when I would wake him up, there was no one else in the bed, except one time when I found Telex, his black Scotty, on his pillow.' General Eisenhower's naval aide, Captain Harry Butcher, told Pinkley that 'Ike worked incessantly, was always protected, always watched. There was no time for an affair.' General Mark Clark, Eisenhower's frequent wartime companion, said 'I never noted anything but friendship between him and Kay.' Journalist Bob Considine, a friend of Summersby, recalled his wife asking directly if she ever slept with General Eisenhower. She replied 'the answer is no. Never if he had asked me, beckoned a finger to me, I would have done anything he asked me to do. But he never asked me.'" Price, "Truth About Gen. Eisenhower," paras. 14, 3–5.

Afterword

cooperative basis and joint activities brought together about 150 denominations ranging from the United Church of Canada, black denominations, Pentecostal and evangelistic organizations, numerous Roman Catholic dioceses and major Protestant church organizations."[5]

With all this excitement as the Jesus movement was expanding from a grassfire movement among the countercultural to a grassroots revival impacting the churches, young pastors were waking up and getting involved. One such young Lutheran pastor, inspired by this moving and shaking elder Lutheran statesman Pastor Bertermann, was Kirkland, Washington's Our Redeemer Lutheran Church's Reverend Bob Rieth, who joined the Fellowship of Christians in the Arts, Media, and Entertainment.

The 1970s, when Pastor Rieth became involved,[6] was a time of constant transition. The United States seemed to be a culture attempting to regain the momentum of the story it was writing about itself and its progress, having been bookended within the violence that confronted the civil rights movement of the 1960s and the increasing clashes over the Vietnam War and its expansion into Cambodia in 1970,[7] culminating in the shooting of twelve Kent State students, with four of them killed, by the National Guard on May 4, 1970. In its present context, the memory of the Pacific Coast's 1966–67 Summer of Love (based in San Francisco's

---

5. Lyon, "Key 73," para. 1.

6. See Jeanne DeFazio's complete interview with Bob Rieth in *Redeeming the Screens*, 152–58, which is excerpted at the beginning of the present book.

7. See Kifner, "4 Kent State Students." The subtitle reads, "8 Hurt in Shooting Follows Reported Sniper at Rally," though Kifner writes, "This reporter, who was with the group of students, did not see any indication of sniper fire, nor was the sound of any gunfire audible before the Guard volley. Students conceding that rocks had been thrown, heatedly denied that there was any sniper," 1. The Kent State protest rally had about 1,000 young people attending, according to Kifner. See also Office of the Historian, "Ending the Vietnam War," for an illuminating explanation of the decisions that caused the expansion of the war and precipitated mass rallies of student protests. For an explanation of how the US became embroiled in the Vietnam conflict in the first place, see McNamara, "Why Did the U.S."

Haight-Ashbury district)[8] had been floating up like flower petals in a wind of change and had sailed away by 1969, a lost bouquet. Bobbing across the nation's consciousness toward the far Atlantic coast, it paused at Max Yasgur's dairy farm in Sullivan County's Woodstock in upper New York as rain and fame dropped on those thirty thousand plus who attended, before it wilted away[9] in the violence yet to come.

In lower New York's Greenwich Village on March 6, 1970, less than a year later, a very different approach was being planned by five wealthy youth in their twenties, three women and two men, all of whom belonged to the radical Weathermen spin-off from the Students for a Democratic Society, which was one of many antiwar student groups among the approximately one million students who disrupted the daily routines of nearly nine hundred college campuses in May of 1970 to protest the expanding of the Vietnam war into Cambodia.[10] Ensconced in a luxurious, parent-owned townhouse, the five young members were making bombs to plant at Columbia University, at Fort Dix in New Jersey, and at several other nearby military targets. When one of them crossed two wires mistakenly, their work exploded, demolishing the house and obliterating three of them so completely the pieces of the bodies took months to identify.[11] Flower power was yielding to explosives, both cerebral and material.

Back before the seventies generation began, in late 1963, Britain's "gift" to the youth of the United States was an invitation to join Beatlemania. Perhaps, if one wanted a single pop-cultural image to capture what was transpiring over the next six years comprising the rest of this decade, the demise of Beatlemania might provide it. Describing its onset, Time Life Books in *This Fabulous Century: 1960–1970* emphasized the positive, infectious quality of

---

8. See Anthony, *Summer of Love*.

9. See Greil Marcus's paean to "The Woodstock Festival: September 1969," in Wenner, *20 Years of Rolling Stone*, 49–56.

10. For more precise details, see Miller, "May 1970 Student Antiwar Strikes."

11. See the fuller description in Jennings and Brewster, *Century*, 423–34.

Afterword

the Beatles' exuberance: "No one proclaimed the message of love and happy living to American youth more beguilingly than four mop-haired rock singers from Liverpool, England, who called themselves The Beatles . . . even referring to explosive subjects like drugs, the four Liverpudlians maintained their endemically light, joyful touch."[12] A mere six years later, although still creating a legacy of beautifully melodic, memorable, and often didactic songs like "All You Need is Love," the band itself broke up in anger in 1969. At its collapse, despite money and adulation from fans still being plentifully bestowed, the bond from the Beatles' youth between two of the leading writers of their songs was demolished. Their disputes had become acrimonious enough to break up the band to the extent that these former friends never completely reunited. Apparently, sadly, and ironically, all they needed was love.

The United States by 1969 was also experiencing a similar lack of national love among its many factions. Strife had created a climate of clashing extremes, wallowing in pleas for peace, while clashing with police in what news journalists Peter Jennings of ABC News and Todd Brewster dubbed the "Years of Doubt 1969–1981."[13]

The impact of such extremes was poignantly reflected in the offerings of the entertainment industry. In the film industry, the five movies nominated for the Academy Award were the winner, *Patton*, followed by *Airport*, *M*A*S*H*, *Tora! Tora! Tora!*, and *Woodstock*. Three of these movies were war movies. All three of these were set in World War II, the last war at that time in which the United States could feel united pride for stopping the Nazis' lethal injustice. By 1970, however, the immediate context was the Vietnam War, where the nation was divided over who exactly was the enemy. That same year, cartoonist Walt Kelly, on a poster condemning littering he had created for Earth Day, put in the mouth of his character Pogo a satirical adaptation of a famous declaration of the War of 1812 that has become iconic: "We have met the

---

12. Time Life Books, *This Fabulous Century*, 18.
13. Time Life Books, *This Fabulous Century*, 18.

enemy and he is us."[14] Apparently, many Americans had begun to feel that way, and not just about pollution.

In the popular music industry, a similar tension was present. In 1970, the top five songs of the year on the *Billboard* charts were led by "Bridge Over Troubled Water," a song about giving support to another. Written by stand-out composer Paul Simon and beautifully sung by Art Garfunkel, Tina Benitez-Eves reports, "Listening to the southern gospel group Swan Silvertones' 1959 song 'Oh Mary Don't You Weep,' one particular line rang out to Simon—*I'll be your bridge over deep water / If you trust in my name*—which helped Simon finish 'Bridge Over Troubled Water,' and its more gospel elements."[15] Many embraced this memorable song as perfect for the time, including Christians, especially after the slogan "Jesus is the bridge over troubled waters" began to appear on posters, returning the reference to Jesus Christ as the original song implied. In the evangelical Presbyterian Church (USA) I was now attending in seminary, Paul Simon's song was sung as "special music" at a Sunday morning worship service by the choir director.

On the *Billboard* charts this piece was followed by the number two song by Burt Bacharach and Hal David (with Cathy Steeves),[16] the yearning-for-love song "(They Long to Be) Close to You," sung by the Carpenters. Songs three and five are what appeared to many to be scathing anti-war songs. One of the four writers of the number three song, "American Woman," and lead singer at the time of Canada's The Guess Who, Burton Cummings, denied the song was anti-United States, despite its lyrics.[17] Burton Cummings was later

---

14. Kelly, "We Have Met." According to an explanation provided by the Billy Ireland Cartoon Library & Museum of the Ohio State University, "During the War of 1812, the United States Navy defeated the British Navy in the Battle of Lake Erie. Master Commandant Oliver Perry wrote to Major General William Henry Harrison, 'We have met the enemy and they are ours.' Kelly's parody of this famous battle report perfectly summarizes mankind's tendency to create our own problems. In this case, we have only ourselves to blame for the pollution and destruction of our environment," para. 2.

15. Benitez-Eves, "Meaning Behind 'Bridge Over Troubled Water,'" para. 2.

16. See Wikipedia, "(They Long To Be) Close to You."

17. See Wikipedia, "American Woman."

Afterword

to become noted among Christians for writing and performing his beautiful song "I'm Scared" about sensing the unsettling presence of God on his eponymous 1976 album on the CBS label Portrait. Motown's Norman Whitfield and Barrett Strong's number five song of the year, "War," performed by Edwin Starr (Charles Edwin Hatcher) was clearly anti-war and to many "a self-evident anti-Vietnam War statement."[18]

Hit song number four, Burt Bacharach and Hal David's "Raindrops Keep Fallin' on My Head," is about adopting a positive attitude to deal with adversity. The theme of this song epitomized similar songs that were to characterize many of the rest of the top recordings of the 1970s, each taking a different attitude toward handling trouble. The 1969 song and its soundtrack both were Oscar winners in their year for the movie *Butch Cassidy and the Sundance Kid*, a tragicomedy drawn from the real lives of two outlaws who could not cope with changing times.

As the seventies rolled on, violent movies continued to be nominated for Oscars like 1971's winner, *The French Connection*, a thriller about the clash between a huge narcotics ring and the police detectives trying to stop it. The runner up, *A Clockwork Orange*, is a futuristic tale about attempts to eradicate the violent tendencies in a British gang who rape and murder each night. The top song of 1971, following the contrasting pattern of "Raindrops Keep Fallin' on my Head," was Three Dog Night's exuberant "Joy to the World"—which, despite its title, has no relation to the classic Christmas hymn.

The Godfather won the Oscar in 1972, while the popular-music-buying public opted for the poignant, romantic "The First Time Ever I Saw Your Face."

The Sting, a lighter comedy about clever con men beating the law and the system earned the Oscar in 1973, while 1973's top Grammy winning "Tie a Yellow Ribbon Round the Ole Oak Tree" by Tony Orlando and Dawn was a hopeful song about an inmate who had not beaten the system, and was just now released from prison, uncertain but receiving a welcome back home.

---

18. Wikipedia, "War (The Temptations Song)," para. 1.

As the mid-seventies were about to arrive, Hollywood persisted in having success with gangster movies, winning again in 1974 with the *Godfather* franchise, *The Godfather Part 2*, while the music industry kept up its own success with the contrasting, moving, and wistful "The Way We Were" by Barbra Streisand.

Another take on crime and its ramifications was 1975's Academy Award-winning *One Flew Over the Cuckoo's Nest*, telling the tale of a small-time criminal trying to avoid jail who feigns insanity only to find the "caretakers" at the hospital where he is incarcerated are out to destroy his independent nature. Again, the number one Grammy winner contrasted with the dark comedic yet tragic Hollywood offering, this time with veteran songwriter Billy Swan's "I Can Help," a rollicking song that carried a similar theme to "Bridge Over Troubled Water," though more buoyant.

By 1976, the Oscar centered on a hero who could survive all the calamity, Sylvester Stallone's masterpiece *Rocky*, a small-time boxer who triumphs over all odds, while the United States record buyers also made a change. They looked outside the USA once again, as they had in the time of the Beatles and the subsequent British Invasion, as the sudden influx of British bands into the US charts was dubbed. This time, however, the public chose for its top song the Swedish group ABBA's "Dancing Queen," a celebration of the thrill of being seventeen.

The pattern was somewhat similar in 1977. Hollywood gave the Oscar to *Annie Hall*, attempting to do, perhaps, for women as *Rocky* did for men, celebrating their struggle, this time in the context of sorting out relationships in the new definition for women the culture was espousing, while dealing with feelings and their neuroses. On its side, the music industry again saw its buyers looking outside the United States, this time to Britain for Rod Stewart's "Tonight's the Night (Gonna Be Alright)," a catchy song whose primary aim was not about promoting women above the traditional level of sex object—but it was British. . .

By 1978, *The Deer Hunter* focused in on the horror of the Vietnam War and the devastation it had caused participants. The number two song of 1977, "I Just Want to be Your Everything,"

Afterword

had been performed by Andy Gibb, younger sibling of the three brothers who formed the enormously successful English trio the BeeGees. His second-place achievement was a prelude to his seizing the top spot in popularity this next year with 1978's number one hit, "Shadow Dancing," a plea to an unrequited love, as the United States continued to look outside, especially once more to the British, for its top inspiration, or commiseration.

1979's *Kramer vs. Kramer* brought alienation home with a family breaking up when a wife leaves to redefine herself and her husband and son find they must do the same. Their attempts precipitate a custody battle for the child. Finally, in 1979, a United States band won back the top of the US charts with New York City's Blondie performing "Heart of Glass," a song band members wrote about disappointment in love, putting film and song themes appropriately side by side.

By 1980, the impact on children heightens with *Ordinary People*, wherein the accidental death of a son triggers a suicide attempt by his brother out of guilt and the progressive disintegration of a family. By that year, ushering in a new decade, the movies selected as runners-up focused on people striving to overcome their limits, afflictions, and the traumas of their backgrounds. *Coal Miner's Daughter* is a biopic dramatizing singer Loretta Lynn's ardent quest to achieve her career in music. *The Elephant Man*, another biopic, followed the grossly deformed John Merrick in his struggle for acceptance. *Raging Bull*, a third biopic, is the round given to Jake LaMotta, a boxer who is portrayed as only able to express himself through violence. Finally, *Tess*, adapted from Thomas Hardy's novel *Tess of the d'Urbervilles*, recounts the woes of a British lower-class girl who is victimized. Again, eerily appropriate, Blondie kept the top music spot for 1980 with the theme song, "Call Me," from the film *American Gigolo*, a story of the plummeting decline of a male prostitute framed for murder, with a final glimmer of pyrrhic hope as a client sacrifices her marriage to rescue him. In this case, one might surmise, symbolically, we in the United States resonated with this sad tale of a failed life, because we were depressed on several counts, feeling deprayed and degraded by the current war into which we had stumbled, and in consternation at the difficulty in ending our own oppression and exclusion of present citizens whom our nation had enslaved for centuries, as well as the culpability of our deceitful treatment of previous inhabitants from whom we siphoned off their land, but hoping for a redemption. At least these are the themes that may have appealed to moviegoers and their critics and pop-music buyers and their critics, assuming the film's attraction was not just the prurient interest of gaping at the male lead's frontal nudity, which was unusual at the time for a mainstream movie.

With all of this cultural context besetting the film and music industries—and we have not talked about the trends in contemporary pictorial art, or dance, or any other art form, but just focused on where the mass attention and money were being invested—the pressures on participants in these two art forms to conform to such trends were increasingly demanding. The way forward appeared to be through embracing national concerns and their moods and trends, since the awards with the garland of their recognition were given to creative films and songs that reflected, responded to, and reacted to national problems. Then, having identified with viewers' and listeners' concerns, celebrated productions could prolong or even dictate further entertainment fads into trends as those employed in these industries sought to emulate the winning and honored films and songs with more offerings that might capture the public and critics' approval.

In such a context, we can see why Bob Rieth's opening years with the Fellowship of Christians in the Arts, Media, and Entertainment were invested in personal evangelism and helping host events that stressed community in bringing celebrities together in Jesus, the only one who can definitively affirm an artist outside of shifting cultures's ephemeral approvals.

In 1981, Dr. Bertermann's involvement in the Fellowship of Christians in the Arts, Media, and Entertainment ended and he died two years later in 1983.

That same year, 1981, showed a completely different Oscar choice: *Chariots of Fire*, an outstanding depiction of the life of the

Afterword

dedicated Christian Eric Liddell, an exemplary Olympic champion who gave up his celebrity to become a missionary and a martyr for his faith in Christ.

All through these years in which we have been considering the impact on the popular arts by reviewing the top grossing commercial and critical choices in movies and popular music, the Jesus movement had been offering a very different message: one of hope, love, and restoration in the sacrificial love of Jesus for humanity.

In the mid-1980s, Bob Rieth, now no longer pastoring a church but concentrating his ministry on his mission to serve journalists and camera crews and other media professionals covering traumatic events, founded with colleagues Media Fellowship International (MFI). An articulate and gifted teacher, Bob was training his friends and new converts to Jesus from his skillful ability to teach the Bible in a way that it impacted lives—in other words, in the way that it should be taught, emulating the power of Jesus's presentations to whichever media/arts population they were called.

Bob's gifts, besides teaching and preaching, included his ability to empower numerous coworkers throughout the entire arts community to bring Bible teachings of encouragement and exhortation to others. One long-term coworker since the 1970s in FCAME is Johnny Probst. Johnny and his wife Patty serve as Chaplains of MFI. They, along with Dr. Susan Stafford and Jeanne DeFazio, the editors of this book, demonstrate that women as well as men were treated as equal coworkers in MFI, reaching out continually, expanding this ministry further by allowing all members to use the gifts the Holy Spirit has given each, as we see explained in 1 Cor 12:7–11.

Clearly, Bob and Johnny and their coworkers did not create a set of subservients, inferior to their leadership, as one sees in cultic groups that undermined the Jesus movement and abused many who trusted them, as, for example, David Berg and his Children of God (aka The Family), under whose command women and children were exploited.[19] Instead, MFI's humble founders were

---

19. See its exploitative tract, "Holy Holes!" by David Berg (who later

Media Fellowship International

recruiting equals in ministry and empowering them to become chaplains to the constituencies they served.

These goals are reflected in their official documents of faith and purpose:

1. Encourage, equip, and energize individuals to live for Christ.
2. Expand the international network of Christians in the media.
3. Encourage interpersonal relationships where Christians can learn how to incorporate their faith into the workplace.
4. Provide information, education, and training to improve professional competencies based on Biblical principles.
5. Provide a platform from which Christians in the media may communicate their faith.[20]

Here we see clearly the goal of empowering others is at the center of each of these statements. We also notice the use of inclusive language. The result is an impressive number of women who have ministered within the many facets of this ministry's outreach.

All of these goals are built on a strong statement of faith. Here are three of its key tenets:

1. The Bible is the inspired, infallible, authoritative word of God.
2. There is one God, eternally existent in three persons—Father, Son, and Holy Spirit.
3. We believe in the deity of our Lord Jesus Christ, in His virgin birth, in His sinless life, in His miracles, in His vicarious and atoning death through His shed blood, in His bodily resurrection, in His Ascension to the right hand of the Father, and in His personal return in power and glory.[21]

---

adopted the name "Moses David") with the photograph of a naked little girl on its first page. Also, to read the heartbreaking reports by some who were molested in this cult, see Hewett and Harrington, "Was the Family Doing God's Work."

20. Media Fellowship International, "MFI Mission Statement," para. 2.
21. Media Fellowship International, "MFI Mission Statement," para. 3.

Afterword

With such a solid foundation, true to its roots, MFI continued its seminal interest: to emphasize serving media journalists and reporters, especially those who are stationed in war zones and other precarious environments through its Media Support Team. As it explains on its website, "The MFI Media Support Team and MST Center exist to offer hospitality and a hand of friendship to the news crews. The Support Team, media professionals themselves, is on location with them, helping them cope with the emotional and physical challenges. This is the need our MFI MST has met in past years. We've been on location in past years to support the Media covering such tragic events as the Oklahoma City bombing, Columbine, Virginia Tech, Katrina, and 9/11 in New York City and Washington, DC, as well as the Atlanta Olympic Bombing."[22] How could the stress, the emotional fatigue, the sense of hopelessness that can afflict those who are reporting disasters and atrocities not be devastating, not just to one's own sense of security but also to one's conscience and compassion? How many journalists enter the inevitable maze that is the question: Could this disaster have been avoided? While search and rescue crews focus on the victims, MFI realizes God cares as well about those of "The 'Media'—the news crews, cameramen, reporters, anchors, technicians. They work under difficult circumstances. They are the first to the scene, the closest to the event—hearing the details of sorrow and anguish—feeling the emotion, fear, and discomfort—yet trying to remain professionally objective and coherent in spite of appalling trauma and disaster."[23]

Inspired with a similar vision to that of Eugene Bertermann before him, Bob Rieth has left an important legacy to continue. At the heart of his motivation, Bob recognized the truth in Isaiah's quoting from the Lord in his Book of Prophecy 55:11, "My word which goes out from my mouth does not return to me without effect [or without success, or in vain, *reqam*]."[24] That word is the en-

---

22. Media Fellowship International, "MFI Media Support Team," paras. 1–2.

23. Media Fellowship International, "MFI Media Support Team," para. 10.

24. Translation of the Hebrew Bible, Masoretic Text (MT) by William

couragement and comfort Bob and his chaplains have conveyed to media specialists swept into the gulf of reporting traumatic events. May this essential ministry continue to flourish.

David Spencer.

About the Authors

Julia C. Davis, EdM from the Harvard Graduate School of Education and an EdM from Bouve College of Health Sciences at Northeastern University. She has held teaching certificates in New York, Massachusetts, and the District of Columbia, and has been certified as an assistant principal and as an assistant special education supervisor. Julia has taught in the public and private sector in community-based programs including METCO, Summer STEP opportunities for underrepresented populations in science and technology, and Head Start. She has served as a member of Parent's Advocacy Group for Massachusetts supporting FAPE and mainstreaming special education students. She has taught pre-K through all twelve grades, adult nonreaders, limited-English-language learners, and GED preparation courses. Julia taught internationally as an undergraduate exchange student in a special education program based in Newnham on Severn, Gloucestershire, England, which operated under the auspices of Antioch College in Ohio. Julia and her husband Dan have three children and three grandchildren. They attend the International Family Church in North Reading, Massachusetts.

Jeanne DeFazio is a former SAG/AFTRA (Screen Actors Guild/American Federation of Television and Radio Artists) actress of Spanish and Italian descent who played supporting parts in theater, movies, and television series, then served the marginalized in the drama of real life. She became a teacher of second-language-learner

About the Authors

children in the barrios of San Diego. She completed a BA in history at the University of California–Davis, an MAR in theology at Gordon-Conwell Theological Seminary, and a Cal State Teach English Language Learners program. From 2009 to the present she has served as an Athanasian Teaching Scholar at Gordon-Conwell's multicultural Boston Campus for Urban Ministerial Education.

The Rev. Dr. William David Spencer is a distinguished adjunct professor of theology and the arts at Gordon-Conwell Theological Seminary's Boston Campus for Urban Ministerial Education. His fifty-eight years of urban ministry include street, music, prison, college chaplaincy, and storefront to seminary educational ministries. He also taught literacy and served as teaching coordinator for Jefferson County, the Kentucky Board of Education's pioneer adult literacy program, where he set up and taught at five Laubach adult literacy and three GED high school equivalency centers. For thirty years he copastored a storefront church in a satellite city of Boston. Honored with several ecclesial and civic awards, two lifetime achievement awards, and twenty writing and editing awards, he is the author of 330 publications, including eighteen books he authored, coauthored, or coedited. Two of his books, *Mysterium and Mystery: The Clerical Crime Novel* and *Chanting Down Babylon: The Rastafari Reader*, are considered the definitive works in their fields. He is the cofounding editor of Wipf and Stock's House of Prisca and Aquila series of egalitarian books, consultant to its Africanus Monograph series and Urban Voice series, and he and his wife, the Rev. Dr. Aída Besançon Spencer, coauthor the monthly blog *Applying Biblical Truths Today* at aandwspencer.blogspot.com, to which they warmly welcome all readers.

Susan Stafford was born in Lynn, Massachusetts, and grew up in Missouri. She started winning beauty contests as a teenager in Kansas City where her modeling career began. Susan moved to California and enjoyed success in costarring roles in major television series and a couple of motion pictures. Susan is best known as the original hostess on *Wheel of Fortune* from 1975 to 1982. She is the first woman ever nominated for an Emmy on a game show, the first woman to get a microphone, and the first woman to make her own clothing deal on a game show. After a trip to India working with Mother Teresa's nuns, Susan was compelled to do more with her life than "turn letters." She left the show and worked for a year as a chaplain intern at a cancer research hospital in Houston and cohosted documentaries about leprosy with former Surgeon General C. Everett Koop and Merlin Olsen. Susan earned a BA in nutrition and an MA and PhD in clinical psychology. She has a degree in theology from Logos International. Susan served on the Emergency Response Team with Media Fellowship International following the school shootings at both Columbine and Virginia Tech, counseling with survivors, family members, and the television crews. Susan worked with Friends of the United Nations and received the World Unity Award for Humanitarian Service along with Edward James Olmos and Martin Luther King III.

By the Same Authors

Julia C. Davis

An Artistic Tribute to Harriet Tubman, with Jeanne DeFazio, editors
The Christian World Liberation Front, contributing author
The Commission, contributing author
Empowering English Language Learners, contributing author
Finding a Better Way, contributing author
Jesus Among the Homeless, contributing author
The Journey Home, contributing author
Otto & The White Dove, contributing author
Specialist Fourth Class John Joseph DeFazio: Advocating for Disabled American Veterans, contributing author

Jeanne C. DeFazio

An Artistic Tribute to Harriet Tubman, with Julia C. Davis, editors
Berkeley Street Theatre: How Improvisation and Street Theater Emerged as Christian Outreach to the Culture of the Time, editor
Christian Egalitarian Leadership, contributing author

By the Same Authors

The Christian World Liberation Front, author

The Commission, editor

Creative Ways to Build Christian Community, with John P. Lathrop, editors

Empowering English Language Learners, with William David Spencer, editors

Finding a Better Way, editor

How to Have an Attitude of Gratitude on the Night Shift, with Teresa Flowers, authors

Jesus Among the Homeless, contributing author

The Journey Home, author

Keeping the Dream Alive: A Reflection on the Art of Harriet Lorence Nesbitt, author and editor

Letting Go, with Terry McDermott, authors

Otto & The White Dove, editor

Redeeming the Screens, with William David Spencer, editors

Specialist Fourth Class John Joseph DeFazio: Advocating for Disabled American Veterans, editor

William David Spencer

Cave of Little Faces, with Aida Besancon Spencer, authors

Chanting Down Babylon, author

Christian Egalitarian Leadership, with Aida Besancon Spencer, editors

Dread Jesus, author

Empowering English Language Learners, with Jeanne C. DeFazio, editors

The Global God, with Aida Besancon Spencer, editors

By the Same Authors

God Through the Looking Glass, author
The Goddess Revival, with Aida Besancon Spencer, editors
Joy Through the Night, with Aida Besancon Spencer, authors
Marriage at the Crossroads with Aida Besancon Spencer, authors
Mystery and Mysterium, author
Name in the Papers, author
Redeeming the Screens, with Jeanne C. DeFazio, editors
Three in One, author

Susan Stafford

The Commission, contributing author
The Journey Home, contributing author
Redeeming the Screens, contributing author
Stop the Wheel, I Want to Get Off, author

Bibliography

ACLU Northern California. "Governor Brown Signs Groundbreaking Data Collection Bill to Combat Racial Profiling." Oct. 3, 2015. https://www.aclunc.org/news/governor-brown-signs-groundbreaking-data-collection-bill-combat-racial-profiling.

Anthony, Gene. *Summer of Love: Haight-Ashbury at Its Highest*. Millbrae, CA: Celestial Arts, 1980.

Benitez-Eves, Tina. "The Meaning Behind 'Bridge Over Troubled Water' by Simon & Garfunkel." American Songwriter, Apr. 14, 2022. https://americansongwriter.com/the-meaning-behind-bridge-over-troubled-water-by-simon-garfunkel/.

Berg, David. *Holy Holes!* GP 237. London: Children of God, 1973.

Bruder, Wally. "My Testimony—Wally Bruder (Pt. 1) 2008." Consumed In Christ, YouTube, Sept. 7, 2008. https://www.youtube.com/watch?v=T0OrETV61TE.

DeFazio, Jeanne C., ed. *Berkeley Street Theatre: How Improvisation and Street Theater Emerged as a Christian Outreach to the Culture of the Time*. House of Prisca and Aquila. Eugene, OR: Wipf & Stock, 2017.

———, ed. *The Commission: The God Who Calls Us to Be a Voice During a Pandemic, Wildfires, and Racial Violence*. Eugene, OR: Wipf & Stock, 2021.

———. "CUME GCTS: 'Creative Ways to Build Christian Community.'" Jeanne DeFazio, YouTube, Oct. 6, 2016. https://www.youtube.com/watch?v=WKRN_XAvwHU.

———. *The Journey Home*. Eugene, OR: Resource, 2024.

———. "Media Fellowship International." In *Redeeming the Screens: Living Stories of Media "Ministers" Bringing the Message of Jesus Christ to the Entertainment Industry*, edited by Jeanne C. DeFazio and William David Spencer, 152–58. House of Prisca and Aquila. Eugene, OR: Wipf & Stock, 2016.

DeFazio, Jeanne C., and John P. Lathrop, eds. *Creative Ways to Build Christian Community*. House of Prisca and Aquila. Eugene, OR: Wipf & Stock, 2013.

DeFazio, Jeanne C., and William David Spencer, eds. *Redeeming the Screens: Living Stories of Media "Ministers" Bringing the Message of Jesus Christ to the Entertainment Industry*. House of Prisca and Aquila. Eugene, OR: Wipf & Stock, 2016.

Bibliography

DeFazio, Jeanne C., et al. "Creative Ways Promo: Susan Stafford, Charlene Eber and Jeanne DeFazio." Jeanne DeFazio, YouTube, Apr. 29, 2021. https://www.youtube.com/watch?v=9KJ_lIbpi_Y.

Eugene R. Bertermann Papers. CN 209. Archives of Wheaton College. https://archives.wheaton.edu/repositories/4/resources/633.

———. M-0002. Concordia Historical Institute. https://concordiahistoricalinstitute.libraryhost.com/repositories/2/resources/480.

Everett, Burgess. "Senators Duel Over 'Race Card.'" Politico, May 22, 2014. https://www.politico.com/story/2014/05/jay-rockefeller-john-johnson-race-106983.

Fellowship of Christians in the Arts, Media, and Entertainment. Box 14, folder 16. Eugene R. Bertermann Papers. Archives of Wheaton College. https://archives.wheaton.edu/repositories/4/archival_objects/107566.

Hewett, Bill, and Maureen Harrington. "Was the Family Doing God's Work—Or Unspeakable Harm?" *People* 64 (2005) 87–90.

Jennings, Peter, and Todd Brewster. *The Century*. New York: Doubleday, 1998.

Kelly, Walt. "We Have Met the Enemy and He Is Us." Earth Day 1970–71 poster, Billy Ireland Cartoon Library & Museum, Ohio State University. https://library.osu.edu/site/40stories/2020/01/05/we-have-met-the-enemy/.

Kifner, John. "4 Kent State Students Killed by Troops." In *The New York Times: The Complete Front Pages, 1851–2008*, 322. New York: Black Dog and Leventhal, 2008.

Lawrence, Keith, and Terry Keleher. "Structural Racism." Race and Public Policy Conference 2004. https://www.intergroupresources.com/rc/Definitions%20of%20Racism.pdf.

Lyon, Randolph W. "Key 73." Encyclopedia Dubuque. https://www.encyclopediadubuque.org/index.php?title=KEY_73.

Marcus, Greil. "The Woodstock Festival: September 1969." In *20 Years of Rolling Stone: What a Long, Strange Trip It's Been*, edited by Jann S. Wenner, 49–56. New York: Friendly, 1987.

Mathis, Wilma Faye. *Jesus Among the Homeless: Successful Strategies of Christian Ministers to the Marginalized*. House of Prisca and Aquila. Eugene, OR: Wipf & Stock, 2023.

McNamara, Robert. "Why Did the U.S. Enter the Vietnam War?" ThoughtCo., updated June 7, 2024. https://www.thoughtco.com/why-did-us-enter-vietnam-war-195158.

Media Fellowship International. "MFI Media Support Team." https://mediafellowship.org/mfi-media-support-team/.

———. "MFI Mission Statement." https://mediafellowship.org/mfi-mission-and-statement-of-faith/.

Miller, Amanda. "May 1970 Student Antiwar Strikes." Mapping American Social Movements Project. https://depts.washington.edu/moves/antiwar_may1970.shtml.

Bibliography

Office of the Historian. "Ending the Vietnam War, 1969–1973." https://history.state.gov/milestones/1969-1976/ending-vietnam.

Pedigo, Sheri. "Sheri Pedigo Reading Her Contribution to *The Commission*." Jeanne DeFazio, YouTube, May 9, 2021. https://www.youtube.com/watch?v=n_hSa2JhgLw.

Price, Doug. "The Truth About Gen. Eisenhower's Alleged Affair During WWII." *Gettysburg Times*, Jun. 11, 2013. https://www.gettysburgtimes.com/opinion/staff_columns/article_4f675bcd-02cb-5caa-8c2f-ace7d2c1bcfo.html.

Rosenwald, Michael S. "Bob Yerkes, Bruised but Durable Hollywood Stuntman, Dies at 92." *New York Times*. Oct. 17, 2024. https://www.nytimes.com/2024/10/17/movies/bob-yerkes-dead.html.

Spencer, Aida Besançon, and William David Spencer, eds. *Christian Egalitarian Leadership: Empowering the Whole Church According to the Scriptures*. House of Prisca and Aquila. Eugene, OR: Wipf & Stock, 2020.

Stafford, Susan. "Aaron Ezra Mann—Producer, Academy Award Winner Is on Out of the Box." Dr. Susan Stafford, YouTube, Apr. 27, 2021. https://www.youtube.com/watch?v=yhUNhi_xmBw.

Stage 32. "Sheri Pedigo." https://www.stage32.com/SheriPedigo.

Time Life Books. *This Fabulous Century: 1960–1970*. This Fabulous Century 7. New York: Time Life Books, 1988.

Valley City Times Record. "Pastor Robert Rieth, 1940–2022." Legacy, Aug. 5–10 2022. https://www.legacy.com/us/obituaries/times-online/name/pastor-robert-rieth-obituary?id=36151990.

The Welsh NHS Confederation. *Arts, Health and Well-Being*. May 2018. https://www.nhsconfed.org/system/files/media/Arts-health-and-wellbeing_0.pdf.

Wenger, Gemma. "Beauty For Ashes—Pastor Gemma Wenger Interviews Martha Reyes of Hosanna Foundation." Gemma Wenger, YouTube, Dec. 24, 2017. https://www.youtube.com/watch?v=Q0DUN4cTrbo.

———. "BFA Show #624." Interview with April Shenandoah. Jeanne DeFazio, YouTube, Oct. 19, 2015. https://www.youtube.com/watch?v=vi7_aqKbOsM.

———. "BFA Show #625." Interview with Bob Rieth. Jeanne DeFazio, YouTube, Oct. 14, 2015. https://www.youtube.com/watch?v=J8b7GYfI_iA.

———. "Gemma Wenger's Beauty for Ashes #613 Jeanne DeFazio re: Creative Ways to Build Christian Community." Jeanne DeFazio, YouTube, Oct. 26, 2015. https://www.youtube.com/watch?v=78JbTZEzZc8.

Wenner, Jann S., ed. *20 Years of Rolling Stone: What a Long, Strange Trip It's Been*. New York: Friendly, 1987.

Wikipedia. "1996 Summer Olympics." Updated Feb. 3, 2025. https://en.wikipedia.org/wiki/1996_Summer_Olympics.

———. "American Woman." Updated Dec. 2, 2024. https://en.wikipedia.org/wiki/American_Woman.

Bibliography

———. "Gemma Wenger." Updated Oct. 31, 2024. https://en.wikipedia.org/wiki/Gemma_Wenger.

———. "(They Long to Be) Close to you." Updated Dec. 8, 2024. https://en.wikipedia.org/wiki/(They_Long_to_Be)_Close_to_You.

———. "War (The Temptations Song)." Updated Nov. 24, 2024. https://en.wikipedia.org/wiki/War_(The_Temptations_song).

Yerkes, Bob. "Bob Yerkes Reading His Contribution to *The Commission*." Jeanne DeFazio, YouTube, May 9, 2021. https://www.youtube.com/watch?v=HmJKCU4ezEM.

www.ingramcontent.com/pod-product-compliance
Lightning Source LLC
Chambersburg PA
CBHW071739090426
42738CB00011B/2529